INFORMATION TECHNOLOGY LAW

WEB LAW: AGREEMENTS, GUIDELINES AND USE POLICIES

LISA K. ABE

MARIE-HÉLÈNE CONSTANTIN

GENERAL EDITOR: SUNNY HANDA

LexisNexis®
Butterworths

Web Law: Agreements, Guidelines and Use Policies

September 2005

Members of the LexisNexis Group worldwide

Canada	LexisNexis Canada Inc, 123 Commerce Valley Drive East, Suite 700, MARKHAM, Ontario
Argentina	Abeledo Perrot, Jurisprudencia Argentina and Depalma, BUENOS AIRES
Australia	Butterworths, a Division of Reed International Books Australia Pty Ltd, CHATSWOOD, New South Wales
Austria	ARD Betriebsdienst and Verlag Orac, VIENNA
Chile	Publitecsa and Conosur Ltda, SANTIAGO DE CHILE
Czech Republic	Orac sro, PRAGUE
France	Éditions du Juris-Classeur SA, PARIS
Hong Kong	Butterworths Asia (Hong Kong), HONG KONG
Hungary	Hvg Orac, BUDAPEST
India	Butterworths India, NEW DELHI
Ireland	Butterworths (Ireland) Ltd, DUBLIN
Italy	Giuffré, MILAN
Malaysia	Malayan Law Journal Sdn Bhd, KUALA LUMPUR
New Zealand	Butterworths of New Zealand, WELLINGTON
Poland	Wydawnictwa Prawnicze PWN, WARSAW
Singapore	Butterworths Asia, SINGAPORE
South Africa	Butterworth Publishers (Pty) Ltd, DURBAN
Switzerland	Stämpfli Verlag AG, BERNE
United Kingdom	Butterworths Tolley, a Division of Reed Elsevier (UK), LONDON, WC2A
USA	LexisNexis, DAYTON, Ohio

Library and Archives Canada Cataloguing in Publication

Abe, Lisa K., 1967-
Web law: agreements, guidelines and use policies / Lisa K. Abe, Marie-Hélène Constantin.

(Information technology law)
Includes index.
ISBN 0-433-44590-4

1. Web sites--Law and legislation--Canada. I. Constantin, Marie-Hélène II. Title. III. Series: Information technology law (Markham, Ont.)

KE452.C6A24 2005 343.7109'944 C2005-905364-X

Printed and bound in Canada.

ABOUT THE AUTHORS

Lisa K. Abe, B.Comm., LL.B., is a partner in the Toronto office of Fasken Martineau LLP. Her practice encompasses information technology development, commercialization, transfer, licensing, procurement, technology-driven merges and acquisitions, IT outsourcing, joint ventures, e-commerce, protection of intellectual property, and other related areas. Ms. Abe is the former Chair of the Toronto Computer Lawyers' Group, is a member of the Ontario Bar Association's Information Technology and E-Commerce Section, the Intellectual Property Institute of Canada, the Computer Law Association, the Canadian IT Law Association and has written and lectured extensively on a broad range of IT issues.

Marie-Hélène Constantin, B.Mus., LL.B., B.C.L., is a lawyer in the Information Technology Group of Blake, Cassels & Graydon LLP, a leading Canadian business law firm. Based in Montreal, Ms. Constantin specializes in technology, intellectual property, privacy, consumer protection, health and language issues, providing commercial and regulatory advice to information technology, pharmaceutical, biotechnology and other companies. Ms. Constantin also practises in the area of employment law. She has published articles and given numerous lectures on privacy, employment, regulatory and information technology issues.

ABOUT THE GENERAL EDITOR

Dr. Sunny Handa is a partner with the international law firm of Blake, Cassels & Graydon LLP and is co-head of the firm's national Information Technology Group. Dr. Handa deals with information technology, intellectual property, e-commerce and communication law matters, and is also Professor of Law (adj.) at McGill University where he teaches in the areas of high technology and intellectual property law. He is the author of *Copyright Law in Canada* and a co-author of *Communications Law in Canada* and *E-Commerce Legislation and Materials in Canada*, all published by LexisNexis Canada, as well as numerous other publications. Dr. Handa also is the creator/developer and General Editor of the Information Technology Law book series and in this role develops, structures and edits each title.

ABOUT THE SERIES

Information Technology Law is an exciting new series of books designed to assist lawyers and business professionals in demystifying complex information technology law issues while requiring no specific prior knowledge on the part of the reader. Each book will focus on a particular cutting edge information technology law subject. The creator and general editor of the series is Dr. Sunny Handa. Each book will be written by different leading Canadian IT jurists with expertise in the particular area. Upcoming titles will cover topics including web agreements and policies, IT outsourcing, open source software, and e-mail. Other titles will continue to be added to the series in coming years.

FOREWORD

This book, the third in the newly minted IT Law Series, is by far the most complex work to-date. Conceptualizing and organizing this book was a great challenge for all three of us at the earliest stages of its development. Lisa and Marie-Hélène have done a wonderful job of taking some very initial and abstract ideas of its organization and scope and have crystalized these ideas into an accessible book that is packed with useful information. The book begins with a discussion of an organization's use of the Web for internal purposes; this is followed by how an organization thinks about administering a Web site; the book then turns to the external use of a Web site (*e.g.*, in selling products and services, etc.) and concludes by discussing various legal and regulatory rules that are increasingly constraining the use of the Web. In other words, it covers the range of legal topics applicable to Web site development and administration.

For those who continue to beat the drum of unbridled Web freedom and the cyber-wild west, this book stands to dispel that myth. The use of the Web for all endeavours, especially those of a commercial nature, is an increasingly difficult and complex proposition; this book guides the user carefully through the applicability of legal rules and procedures when navigating through cyberspace. Any organization using the Web, no matter what its use, would do well to familiarize itself with the content of this book.

In terms of the genesis of this book project, it began with a discussion that Marie-Hélène and I had two years ago. She and I have worked together as colleagues for the past eight years and I have watched her develop a wonderful expertise in dealing with electronic commerce and Web issues. In fact, I had seen so many of her presentations and read so many of her memos and letters that I mentioned to her that these should form the basis of a book project. We quickly brought in our colleague, Lisa Abe, who is an accomplished author in her own right and who had been writing in the same field. Interestingly, during the writing of this book, Lisa decided to leave the firm that the three of us were working at, and moved to the firm from whence Marie-Hélène and I came some three years back. It was a trade of IT lawyers of sorts. That said, we had three years of overlap where we worked together and became good friends.

Although difficult to craft, I think this book represents an easily accessible and enjoyable read while simultaneously imparting a great amount of detailed legal information on Web law.

Sunny Handa
September 1, 2005

PREFACE

This book forms part of the series entitled "Information Technology Law in Canada", edited by Dr. Sunny Handa. This series is designed to provide a collection of affordable, yet comprehensive, texts dealing with information technology law on an ongoing basis. Each book in the series deals with a particular aspect of information technology law; some texts are more oriented to legal subject-matter, whereas others focus on particular applications, sometimes referred to as an industry focus.

This book belongs in the latter category, as it deals with a variety of legal subjects with two common threads: (i) the use of the World Wide Web and the legal issues surrounding the structuring of Web Sites by individuals and organizations and (ii) the contractual terms, sometimes in the form of terms of use or online agreements and at other times in the form of policies or procedural guidelines, used in these circumstances. These policies cover both the use of the Internet (or other types of computer networks) and the administration of the Web sites themselves.

We wish to acknowledge and thank all those who assisted us with this work, and in particular our assistants, Danielle Côté and Rosemary McLaughlin, as well as Patrick Kergin and Jeanne Morency of Blake, Cassels & Graydon LLP and Eva Harris of Fasken Martineau DuMoulin LLP. We also wish to thank Dr. Sunny Handa for his great patience and invaluable support in the completion of this work. We both had the joy of working with Sunny over the years and appreciate his unique energy and outlook.

On a more personal note, we would also like to thank our families and friends for their unfailing support in the pursuit of this project. Finally, we wish to thank each other for tirelessly working to complete this book in the allotted time while maintaining busy practices.

We wish to remind the reader that the comments contained herein are entirely our own and do not reflect those of the firms for which we work. Further, prior to relying on any of the material contained in this book, readers should double-check the material and seek appropriate legal counsel where necessary.

Marie-Hélène Constantin

Lisa Abe

TABLE OF CONTENTS

TABLE OF CASES

C

D

F

G

H

INTRODUCTION

Having a presence on, or access to, the World Wide Web is an essential part of doing business both with respect to external players and in terms of communicating within an enterprise. However, such a presence may subject an organization to a number of laws both in Canada and elsewhere. The focus of this book is to outline Canadian laws that impact Web-based activities and to provide organizations with strategies for the development of Web policies that will help to ensure compliance with Canadian Web laws, including discussion on the issues and terms that should be addressed in such policies and how an organization's Web policies should be structured and implemented to maximize enforceability and benefit. This book will address not just the laws and issues arising in Canada's common law provinces and territories, but also the civil law as it applies within the Province of Quebec.

Establishing and enforcing clear Web policies can benefit an organization in many ways. In an employment context, employees are made aware of what is expected of them and the employer can establish cause for discipline under Canadian employment laws, if policies have not been complied with. They also constitute an important tool for the organization in protecting the confidentiality of its information.

In the context of the development, operation and maintenance of an organization's Web site, Web site administration policies can ensure that the organization complies with Canadian Web laws and that best practices are implemented consistently across the organization to minimize the risks of having a Web presence. In conducting Web commerce, Web policies that supplement Web agreements can help to reduce liability risk for Web site owners, Web providers, Webmasters, Webauthors, content providers, and other participants in the Internet community. As well, online Web policies can serve as tools to achieve legislative or regulatory compliance and can help to promote customer confidence and trust.

When addressing the wide topic of policies, guidelines and agreements that may be drafted and adopted by organizations, it becomes necessary to divide the topic into manageable issues. Although these divisions are somewhat arbitrary, this book will start by addressing first the policies and guidelines that may be adopted by organizations in dealing with its members, which we have named "Internal Policies" for the purposes of this book.

We will start by addressing issues that arise in providing to members of organizations the tools to have access and communicate on the Web, as well as provide guidelines in drafting policies to manage these issues, based on the legal principles that will be briefly outlined. The chapter, entitled "World Wide Web", will explore in more details the issues of monitoring of the use of technological tools by employees or other users and their expectation of privacy.

We will then explore issues related to the adoption of an intranet (or internal network) by an organization. In this context, we address two issues, namely the risks of disclosure of confidential information as well as the policies and practices that should be adopted to reduce such risks, and the posting of personal information on such intranet. The issues explored in that section (Chapter 2) are also applicable in other contexts, such as to the disclosure of confidential information through an organization's Web site or to the collection of personal information of its clients by an organization. In order to limit the length of this book and avoid unnecessary repetition, references to these sections will be found in other relevant chapters of this book.

PART 1

INTERNAL COMPANY POLICIES

This Part will address the policies and guidelines that may be adopted by an organization in dealing with its members; we begin by addressing issues that arise in providing to members of organizations the tools to have access and communicate on the Web. We will also provide guidelines in drafting policies to manage these issues, based on the legal principles that will be briefly outlined.

1

WORLD WIDE WEB

This chapter focuses on policies related to the internal management of a company or other organization in relation to its employees' use of employer-provided Web access. This chapter also briefly highlights some of the key risks associated with Web access and the use of external e-mail by employees. In addition, the limits set out by law with regard to the employer's right to review and control such activities will be explored. Finally, practical solutions that may be implemented by employers to deal with these issues will be presented, including with respect to the communication and implementation of Internet and e-mail use policies as well as the content of such policies.

This chapter also discusses privacy principles that apply in the employment context and the monitoring of the use of technological tools by employees, as such principles have been applied in Canada; because of the scope of such activities, it serves as a guide and is not meant to be all-inclusive. Accordingly, employers should ensure that they obtain appropriate legal advice based on their particular fact situation prior to taking any action against or imposing any sanction on an employee who acts in breach of the principles outlined in the present text or in violation of an Internet or e-mail use policy put in place by an employer.

I. THE RISKS FACED BY EMPLOYERS FOR WEB ACCESS BY EMPLOYEES

Although many types of risks may be associated with an employee's use of his or her employer's Internet connection, some common types of risks may be identified. First, there is a risk of financial loss for the organization. This risk may take many forms, but loss of productivity is perhaps the most obvious. According to a survey conducted in the United States in 2001, 34 per cent of companies had reprimanded or disciplined employees for inappropriate use of the Internet.[1] In 2002, a similar survey indicated that employees averaged 8.3 hours per week accessing non-work related Web sites, such as sites dedicated to shopping, news, pornography,

---

[1] David Greenfield, web@work Employer Survey 2001 = Termination and Litigation, online: <http://www.websense.com/company/news/research/webatwork2002.pdf> (last accessed on August 23, 2004).

gambling and online auctions.[2] Another risk of direct financial loss for an organization is the risk of damages to its products or equipment, for example, through the introduction of viruses into the organization's information technology systems.

A second type of risk associated with granting Internet access to employees relates to the potential loss of a competitive advantage for the organization. This risk is largely associated with the possible disclosure of confidential information or trade secrets by employees when using, for example, chat sites, or when sending e-mail. This may lead to a loss of profit and of reputation due to the potential leakage of corporate information or trade secrets.

Finally, there is a risk of liability for the organization, such as for contractual violations, intellectual property rights infringement, defamation, harassment or discrimination claims, unauthorized disclosures or even potential criminal liability as a result of an employee's conduct on the Web.

A given situation may easily fall into more than one of the categories outlined above. For example, an employee may bind the employer by entering into contracts and, in so doing, create a risk of contractual liability for the organization. Furthermore, the type of contract entered into can then create additional risks; the following situation illustrates this idea. In the case of a software development company that grants Internet access to its employees, a programmer wishing to find a solution to a programming problem (or simply to save time) may access open source code available on the Internet, download such source code and integrate it into the employer's software in development. Open source code is usually the subject of licence agreements. In downloading this software, the employee may have agreed to be bound by the terms of a licence agreement, and the employer may find itself bound, vicariously, by the terms of this licence. Such terms may include, for example, the obligation to render the source code of all software into which the open source code has been integrated available to the public. This obligation may bind the employer to make the source code of its organization's software product available to the public as open source code. This could result in a significant loss of future revenue and opportunities to the employer.

These risks arise because: (i) information can be communicated much more quickly, freely and easily through the use of computer networks than through traditional means; and (ii) individuals tend to have

2 Harris Interactive Inc., web@work Survey 2002 = Cyber-Addiction in the Workplace, online: <http://www.websense.com/company/news/research/webatwork-employer2002.pdf> (accessed on August 23, 2004).

a more casual approach when engaging in correspondence, discussions, or even entering into agreements electronically. In addition, electronic communications have fostered an environment where anonymity or the impersonation of a third party is increasingly common place and sometimes used to conduct fraudulent business, to harass individuals or to communicate offensive messages.

II. MONITORING AND PRIVACY

In order to limit the risks outlined above, an employer may wish to monitor the use of the communication tools that it makes available to its employees, such as Web access, e-mail and other technologies. However, is there a legal right for an employer to do so and, if so, what are the limits of such a right? The monitoring by an employer of the conduct of employees is limited by the employees' right to privacy. Although no simple and concise definition of the right to privacy exists, in the context of this chapter, privacy will be defined generally as the right to be left alone or the right to exercise control over one's personal information.[3]

As it will be outlined below through an examination of the relevant legislative provisions and case law, an employer may have the right to exercise such monitoring in certain circumstances. The scope of this right to monitor the employees conduct varies on the basis of the specific facts of each case. It is therefore important to understand the legal principles at play. In addition, one important factor in evaluating the facts of each case will be the existence of a well-drafted and appropriately publicized and enforced policy on the use of technological tools by employees. We will therefore briefly explore the relevant legislative provisions and past case law in order to enable organization to draft policies appropriate for their purposes and will provide tips as to the content and enforcement of such policies.

In the legislative context, the right to privacy is enshrined in various pieces of legislation, such as the *Canadian Charter of Rights and Freedom*[4] (s. 8, Search and Seizure and s. 7, Liberty), the Canadian *Criminal Code*[5] (Interception of Private Communications), various international conventions, the *Personal Information Protection and Electronic Documents Act*[6]

---

[3] In *R. v. Duarte*, [1990] S.C.J. No. 2, [1990] 1 S.C.R. 30, the Supreme Court of Canada defined privacy as "the right of the individual to determine when, how, and to what extent he or she will release personal information".

[4] Part I of the *Constitution Act, 1982*, being Schedule B to the *Canada Act 1982* (U.K.), 1982, c. 11 ("Canadian Charter").

[5] *Criminal Code*, R.S.C. 1985, c. C-46.

[6] S.C. 2000, c. 5 ("*PIPEDA*").

and other privacy and personal data protection legislation, both at the federal or provincial level.

The Supreme Court of Canada has also provided guidelines with regard to the scope of the right to privacy. These guidelines, although provided in the context of criminal law and search and seizure cases, may nonetheless be applied in the private context as will be outlined later in this chapter. The Supreme Court of Canada has also developed the principle of one's reasonable expectation of privacy as a standard against which government action is to be measured in the criminal law and search and seizure context.

The section that follows will, first, present the legislative structure and, second, discuss the jurisprudential context regarding the right to privacy in Canada, in order to better understand the limits imposed on an employer's right to monitor its employees' Web access and use of electronic mail provided by the employer.

A. Legislative Protection of Individual Privacy Rights

The right to the respect of one's private life has been recognized as a fundamental right by the courts in Canada for some time, even in the absence of specific legislation to that effect.[7] Today, the concerns of the general population regarding the protection of one's private life are reflected in both federal and provincial legislation.

1. Federal

(a) Canadian Charter

Since the enactment of the *Canadian Charter* in 1982, the rights and freedoms of individuals have been of significant interest to the Canadian legal community. The right to privacy is often examined in cases dealing with s. 8 of the *Canadian Charter* that grants to every person the right to be protected against unreasonable search and seizure. However, by virtue of its s. 32, the application of the *Canadian Charter* is limited to cases involving state action and it cannot be invoked in the realm of private litigation. Regardless of this limitation, the Supreme Court of Canada has clearly indicated that common law principles in cases involving private actors should be developed and applied by the courts in a manner that

---

[7] *Hunter v. Southam Inc.*, [1984] 2 S.C.R. 145.

echoes the fundamental values of the *Canadian Charter.*[8] Therefore, with regard to privacy issues in the employment context, any search or seizure by an employer of an employee, or of an employee's property, must be reasonable.[9] This standard would likely also apply to searches of an employee's e-mail, voice mail, computer system or Internet use (to the extent that such items are considered the employee's property).

(b) Interception of Communications

Another relevant element of the protection of the right to privacy is found in the *Criminal Code*, since a person may incur criminal liability for the violation of an individual's right to privacy. For example, according to s. 184 of the *Criminal Code,*[10] a person who wilfully intercepts another's private communication (such as a telephone conversation) is guilty of a criminal offence and liable to imprisonment for a term of up to five years. This example could apply, in the employment context, to the interception by an employer of the private communication of one of its employees. A "private communication" is defined by the *Criminal Code* as any oral communication, or any telecommunication, made by a person under circumstances in which it is reasonable for that person to expect that the communication will not be intercepted by anyone other than the person he or she is in communication with.[11] In other words, a private communication may only be intercepted when either the originator of the private communication or the recipient has consented to an interception of the private communication and the required authorization to that effect has been obtained.[12]

(c) Personal Information Legislation

The *Personal Information Protection and Electronic Documents Act,*[13] or *PIPEDA*, governs the collection, use and disclosure of personal information by certain organizations. Issues arising under this legislation

---

8 *R.W.D.S.U., Local 580 v. Dolphin Delivery Ltd.*, [1986] S.C.J. No. 75, [1986] 2 S.C.R. 573.

9 In *Re Doman Forest Products and I.W.A., Loc. 1-357* (1990), 13 L.A.C. (4th) 275 (B.C.), Arbitrator Vickers cite *Dolphin Delivery* and goes on to applies the *Canadian Charter*'s values to a labour dispute.

10 *Criminal Code*, R.S.C. 1985, c. C-46.

11 *Ibid.*, s. 183.

12 According to s. 184.2(3) of the *Criminal Code*, *ibid.*, such authorization may be given if the judge to whom the application is made is satisfied that there are reasonable grounds to believe that an offence has been or will be committed, that either the originator of the private communication or the person intended by the originator to receive it has consented to the interception, and that there are reasonable grounds to believe that information concerning an offence will be obtained through the interception.

13 S.C. 2000, c. 5.

will be examined further in the chapter 2 of this book dealing with Intranet-related issues. However, for the purposes of this review of privacy-related legislation, it is important to point out that the *PIPEDA* has been applied to cases where employers have used various technologies to monitor activities of employees.[14]

2. Provincial

(a) Civil Liability for Invasion of Privacy

The right to privacy is now also increasingly recognized in a civil context. In common law provinces, the right to privacy in tort is slowly emerging as an independent tort, separate from the torts of trespass or nuisance. At least four provinces, British Columbia,[15] Manitoba,[16] Newfoundland,[17] and Saskatchewan,[18] have enacted legislation creating the tort of invasion of privacy. These Acts consider that the audio or video surveillance, the interception of a conversation spoken trough telecommunication, the unauthorized use of a person's letters, diaries or other personal documents, and the unauthorized use of the name, likeness or voice of a person for the purpose of advertising or for any other purpose of gain if the person is identifiable, as *prima facie* evidence of a violation of privacy.

The *Civil Code of Quebec* also contains several provisions granting to every person the right to the respect of his or her reputation of privacy.[19]

(b) Quebec Legislation on the Privacy Rights of Employees

In addition, the Province of Quebec has enacted specific legislative provisions concerning the privacy rights of employees. According to these provisions,[20] an employer is bound "to take any measures consistent with the nature of the work to protect the health, safety and dignity of the employee". The violation of an employee's privacy (through the

---

14 See, for example, Commissioner's Findings, *PIPEDA* case summary #264: Video cameras and swipe cards in the workplace, Privacy Commissioner of Canada, online: <http:www.privcom.gc.ca/cf-dc/2004/cf-dc_040219_01_e.asp> (date accessed: July 7, 2004).

15 *Privacy Act*, R.S.B.C. 1996, c. 373.

16 *Privacy Act*, C.C.S.M. c. P125.

17 *Privacy Act*, R.S.N.L. 1990, c. P-22.

18 *The Privacy Act*, R.S.S. 1978, c. P-24.

19 Articles 35-41 of the *Civil Code of Quebec*, S.Q. 1991, c. 64 ("C.C.Q").

20 Article 2087 C.C.Q.

monitoring of private telephone conversations, voice messages, e-mail communications, etc.) could arguably constitute an affront to this dignity.

The employees' right to privacy is further protected by legislative provisions providing that evidence is inadmissible if it was obtained in a manner that violated a fundamental right and if its use would tend to bring the administration of justice into disrepute.[21] Consequently, if a court finds that an employee's right to privacy has been violated, for example, by the interception of his or her e-mail messages, the evidence of this employee's wrongdoing obtained through such a violation of privacy may not be admissible in court.

In addition, s. 46 of the Quebec's *Charter of Human Rights and Freedom*[22] indicates that "[e]very person who works has a right, in accordance with the law, to fair and reasonable conditions of employment which have proper regard for his health, safety and physical well-being". This provision has been invoked,[23] although not always successfully,[24] to contest the use of surveillance of employees by an employer, whether by video or otherwise. It may therefore be possible to argue by analogy in certain circumstances that the monitoring of an employee's telephone conversations or Internet use constitutes an unfair and unreasonable working condition. If the court finds that there has been a violation of the privacy of an employee, the victim is entitled to obtain the cessation of the violation, as well as compensation for any moral or material prejudice resulting from the violation. If the violation is intentional, the payment of punitive damages may also be ordered.[25]

B. The Impact of the Legislation on Workplace Technologies

The case law has attempted to balance the competing interests of employers and employees and has sometime examined more specifically the impact of these competing interests on the use of workplace technologies. Although many older cases dealing with the use of technology in the workplace have focused on the use of video surveillance, the principles regarding the right to privacy that have evolved from that jurisprudence can be applied by analogy to other technologies. We will begin by examining the principles established by the Supreme Court of Canada

---

21 *Ibid.*, Art. 2858.

22 R.S.Q. c. C-12 ("*Quebec Charter*").

23 *Paquin v. Distribution Nadair Ltée*, D.T.E. 92T-905 (C.T.).

24 *Centre local de services communautaires Gaston-Lessard* and *Fédération de la santé et des services sociaux (C.S.N.)*, D.T.E. 2000T-564 (T.A).

25 *Charter of Human Rights and Freedom*, R.S.Q. c. C-12, s. 49.

with respect to the protection of privacy, and briefly discuss the general issue of search and seizure in the employment context. We will then review the key principles emerging from the most important cases relating to video surveillance in the employment context and the case law on electronic monitoring in order to extract some general principles; these will allow us to formulate practical solutions on how employers can develop policies to deal with the issue of control and use of new technologies while still respecting the employees' right to privacy.

1. The Supreme Court of Canada's Vision of Privacy

The Supreme Court of Canada in *Hunter v. Southam*[26] stated that s. 8 of the *Canadian Charter* guarantees broad constitutional protection against unreasonable search and seizure extending at least so far as to protect the right to privacy of an individual from unjustified state intrusion. The Supreme Court established, in that case, the principle of "reasonable expectation of privacy" as a standard against which government action should be examined. According to this standard, a person's right to privacy is defined by what that person reasonably expects to be considered private. This same standard was later adopted in the employment law context in cases of video surveillance, as discussed below.

The Supreme Court of Canada was also asked to define the scope of the right to privacy further in subsequent cases.[27]

For example,[28] the Supreme Court examined a situation where a police officer obtained a blood sample from a doctor who was treating an emergency patient without first obtaining the patient's consent. This behaviour was held to be a violation of the patient's privacy and thus constituted an unlawful search and seizure in violation of s.8 of the *Canadian Charter*. The Supreme Court also stated that privacy rights could be physical, territorial and informational.

In the landmark decision of *R. v. Duarte*,[29] the Supreme Court illustrated the concept of the reasonable expectation of privacy in the context of audio surveillance. In that case, the police proceeded with surveillance of a conversation, without court authorization, but with the consent of one of the parties to the conversation. The Court found that this surreptitious surveillance by the stated constituted a violation of privacy and an

26 [1984] 2 S.C.R. 145.

27 See for example *R. v. Stewart*, [1988] S.C.J. No. 45, [1988] 1 S.C.R. 963.

28 *R. v. Dyment*, [1988] S.C.J. No. 82, [1988] 2 S.C.R. 417.

29 *R. v. Duarte*, [1990] S.C.J. No. 2, [1990] 1 S.C.R. 30.

unreasonable search and seizure under s. 8 of the *Canadian Charter*. The Supreme Court later extended this principle to cover video surveillance.[30]

It is also interesting to note the case of an Internet service provider (ISP) of the Province of Alberta that discovered, during the course of a routine repair of an electronic mailbox, attachments to an e-mail message that appeared to contain child pornography. The ISP informed the police and forwarded the message to the police, at its request. The trial judge found that e-mail held by an ISP carries a reasonable expectation of privacy and, therefore, judicial pre-authorization (a warrant) will usually be required to search and seize it. This decision of the trial judge was confirmed by the Alberta Court of Appeal.[31]

The burden of establishing that a reasonable expectation of privacy exists is borne by the person invoking it and the determination of whether such a reasonable expectation of privacy exists is made on the basis of the totality of the circumstances of each case, including the location and the purpose(s) of the intrusion.[32]

These decisions, rendered under the *Canadian Charter*, do not directly apply to the private sector but are only aimed at state action. The Supreme Court's analysis of the concept of privacy is nonetheless important as it establishes a standard for measuring whether an invasion of privacy has occurred.

2. Privacy in the Employment Context

As stated earlier, legislative provisions also protect the right to privacy of individuals in the employment context. Consequently, an employer that attempts to monitor or control an employee's Web access and e-mail use by accessing the personal computer files, e-mail messages and voice mail of an employee, or to monitor an employee's controlling remote or external access or by performance through the use of Web cameras, may be violating that employee's right to privacy.

An employer does not have a general right to conduct such searches of areas that may be considered as within the sphere of privacy of the individual employee. However, this sphere of privacy may be reduced through certain conduct of the employer. For example, the employer may include, in its standard employment contract, a clause that establishes the

---

30 *R. v. Wong*, [1990] S.C.J. No. 118, [1990] 3 S.C.R. 36.

31 *R. v. Weir*, [1998] A.J. No. 155, 59 Alta. L.R. (3d) 319 at para. 70 (Q.B.), affd [2001] A.J. No. 869, 156 C.C.C. (3d) 188 (C.A.).

32 *R. v. Edwards*, [1996] S.C.J. No. 11, [1996] 1 S.C.R. 128; *R. v. Colarusso*, [1994] S.C.J. No. 2, [1994] 1 S.C.R. 20.

right of the employer to monitor the use of technologies tools (such as e-mail) by the employee. The employee is therefore warned of possible searches and of their scope, and essentially, limits his or her expectation of privacy by entering into the employment contract.

The employment contract may also contain a clause stating that, by entering into the contract, the employee will be bound by all of the employer's policies, of which the employee has received a copy. The employment contract will, therefore, incorporate by reference the employer's policies. Employers will also often institute Web Policies as discussed below in Section III "Practical Solutions and Considerations" regulating Web access or e-mail use by employees. Typically, these policies reserve the right of the employer to search, consult and collect information on an employee's computer. In that case, the policies establishing the rights to search e-mails and files of employees form part of the conditions of employment and also serve to limit the scope of an employee's expectation of privacy.

In addition to expressly consenting to such monitoring, an employee may have given implied consent to this conduct by the employer. Implied consent is consent that may be inferred from the conduct of the parties. For example, if the employee is aware that the employer has proceeded with monitoring of Internet use in the past, so as to establish what amounts to a common practice, this monitoring may be implicitly authorized. Such a practice must have been uniformly and consistently applied, and would amount to a condition of employment known to the employees. In a situation where the employer's policies are not part of the terms of employment found in an agreement, implied consent may sometimes nonetheless be inferred from the existence and application of these policies, if there is evidence of a "practice" showing that the policies are known to the employees and are consistently applied. Other circumstances can also give rise to an employer's right to monitor the use of technologies tools it provides to its employees, as will be seen below.

(a) Public vs. Private Settings

The principles developed by the Supreme Court of Canada have led to the emergence of the important concept of an individual's reasonable expectation of privacy as applied in the employment context. The case law first evolved in the context of video surveillance of employees and indicated that such surveillance in a public context generally does not violate an employee's right to privacy, whereas the surveillance of an employee in a private setting is unacceptable. However, the workplace is in many ways a hybrid of the public and private settings. The main factors to take into consideration to determine whether an employee can reasonably expect a certain level of privacy in a given situation are therefore those of public areas versus private settings or areas. When an employee is acting in a public setting or area, it would be unreasonable for such an employee to expect a high level of privacy. This concept applies to situations which take place both inside and outside the workplace.[33]

Monitoring an employee's activities in the workplace by the use of technology does not necessarily violate the employee's right to privacy since the employee's actions while performing his or her duties do not form part of the employee's private life.[34] The workplace is, for the most part, considered to be a public setting. However, surveillance in the workplace can still violate an employee's privacy if it was reasonable, in the circumstances, for the employee to expect his or her privacy to be respected.[35]

The jurisprudence on Web access and e-mail use monitoring by employers has logically evolved from the jurisprudence on video surveillance in the workplace. In fact, the general principles and limitations applicable to the employer's right to monitor employees by video cameras can be applied to monitoring using computer software or other new technologies. The principle of an employee's reasonable expectation of privacy is still

---

33 For example, video surveillance carried out on public property (not on the employer's premise) where the employee was subject to public scrutiny was held to be reasonable; see *Walbar Canada Inc and United Steelworkers of America, Local 9236*, (April 22, 1993), unreported.

34 *Société des alcools du Québec v. Syndicat des employés de magasins et de bureaux de la Société des alcools du Québec*, [1983] T.A. 335 at 336 ("SAQ").

35 In *Richardson v. Davies Wire Industries Ltd.*, [1997] B.C.J. No. 937 (S.C.), the British Columbia Supreme Court also found that an employee "could not reasonably expect to have the protection of privacy when he was sleeping on company time, on company property, and in circumstances where he could be expected to be contacted if needed"; see also *Bombardier v. Association internationale des machinistes et des travailleurs de l'aérospatiale, loge avionnière de Montréal, loge 712*, D.T.E. 96T-375 (T.A.); in this case, the employer's toilet, located in the workplace, had been intentionally plugged up with toilet paper on a number of occasions. The employer repaired the damage and attempted to solve the matter is various ways, but could not find the culprit and the vandalism continued to occur. After having tried various other solutions to no avail, the employer installed video cameras, including one that could be used to identify the employee entering the toilet and one inside the cubicle, placed in such a way that the person inside could not be seen but the roll of toilet paper could be captured on camera. From the video, it could be determined that one employee unrolled several feet of toilet paper and blocked the toilet. The employee argued that the videotape was inadmissible as evidence since it constituted a violation of his right to privacy and dignity. The arbitrator found that, although an employee could normally have a high expectation of privacy in a washroom, some factors could reduce that expectation of privacy. In this case, given the recent repairs done in the washroom by the employer, and since employees knew that the employer was closely following the vandalism problem, employees could not effectively argue a violation of privacy. The arbitrator recognized that this was a situation of necessity, where the use of video camera was the only way that the source of the problem could be identified. Other alternatives, such as placing a security guard in the bathroom to monitor the employees, would have constituted an abuse of rights.

the key to determine whether the employer can assert its right to monitor its employees' work over their right to privacy.

Under certain circumstances, the employer may have the right to monitor its employees' work electronically, in particular where the employees have a low expectation of privacy. Many cases support the proposition that when the computer equipment belongs to the employer and the work was done in the workplace during work hours, the employer has the right to verify that its computers are being used to do useful work that meets the employer's objectives.[36] For example, the employer may wish to claim such a low expectation of privacy to justify a search of the hard drive of an employer-owned computer being used by an employee, in order to ensure that it is used for work-related purposes and that Web access for illegal or immoral purposes is not occurring. In one case, an employer, after having advised an employee verbally many times and even after having sent a letter of reprimand, discovered that the employee was still using the employer's computer to access non-work-related Web sites, such as dating Web sites and pornographic Web sites. In that case, the employer's search of the computer being used by the employee was found not to be in breach of the employee's right of privacy.[37]

As well, if an employee posts a message from a computer belonging to his or her employer on a discussion board on the employer's network, such employee cannot reasonably expect that this message will remain private. The employer can read the message and issue disciplinary sanction if the employee breached his or her obligation of loyalty or duty of fidelity.[38] Some case law also supports the argument that it is unreasonable for an employee to expect privacy in respect of documents that were produced on the employers computers and copied into the employer's main frame computer through the employer's network.[39] Presumably such reasoning would also extend to the copying of such information to any other type of employer computer server.

In the modern working environment, more and more employees are also being remotely connected to their employers and are not actually carrying out their activities "in the workplace" in the traditional sense. It

---

36 *Alliance de la fonction publique du Canada et Musée des beaux-arts du Canada* (2003), RJDT 468 (T.A); *Association des professionnels de la Régie régionale de la santé et des services sociaux 002 (CSN) et Régie régionale de la santé et des services sociaux du Saguenay-Lac St-Jean* (2002), RJDT 990 (T.A.).

37 *Musée, ibid., Blais c. Société des loteries vidéos du Québec* (2003), RJDT 261.

38 *Camosun College v. Canadian Union of Public Employees, Local 2081(Metcalfe grievance),* [1999] BCCAAA No. 490.

39 *International Association of Bridge, Structure and Ornemental Ironworkers Local Union 97 and Office and Technical Employees Union Local 15,* [1997] BCCAAA No. 630.

will be interesting to see how the courts will apply this concept of private versus public setting when confronted with such a situation.

(b) Necessity

Another factor that has been taken into account by the courts is that of necessity.[40] For example, when an employer had no alternative other than to monitor his employees by the use of cameras, arbitrators have allowed surveillance and monitoring. Situations where monitoring is considered necessary may therefore arise where theft or other crimes occurred on the employer's property.

The particular circumstances of the each situation will have to be examined to determine if a conduct constitutes a violation of the right to privacy. Given that the legislation does not set up an absolute prohibition against violations of privacy, it is essential to assess the totality of the circumstances before undertaking any conduct that could constitute a violation of an employee's right to privacy. As outlined above, monitoring can be legitimate when particular circumstances justify it or render it necessary.

(c) Breach of Duty

Employees have a duty of fidelity or of loyalty to their employer. Consequently, dishonesty can be the cause of a lawful termination of employment.[41] Given the nature of this relationship, an employer may monitor an employee it has reasons to believe that the employee is violating his or her duty of loyalty or fidelity. In fact, where an employer suspects that an employee might be dishonest, the monitoring of this employee can serve to gather evidence in order to fulfil the legal requirement needed for terminating the employee with cause.[42]

(d) Limits of the Right to Monitor

As previously stated, the monitoring by an employer of its employees is limited to areas where the employee has no reasonable expectation of privacy.[43] For example, as illustrated by the case law of video surveillance,

---

40 *Bombardier v. Association international des machinistes et des travailleurs de l'aérospatiale, loge avionnière de Montréal, loge 712,* D.T.E. 96T-375 at 26, 36 (T.A.).

41 Article 2088 C.C.Q.; *McKinley v. BC Tel,* [2001] S.C.J. No. 40, [2001] 2 S.C.R. 161.

42 *Richardson v. Davies Wire Industries Ltd., C. U. P.W., Calgary Local No. 710 v. (Canada Post Corp.),* [1987] A.J. No. 452, [1987] 5 W.W.R. 262 (Q.B.).

43 Privacy Commissioner, *PIPEDA* case summary #264: Video camera and swipe cards in the work place, Privacy Commissioner of Canada, online: <http://www.privcom.gc.ca/cf-dc/2004/cf-dc_040219_01_e.asp> (date accessed: July 7, 2004).

an employer is generally not allowed to place Web cameras in the employees' lounge, washrooms, and changing facilities. Moreover, the Web cameras could generally not be used to manage the productivity of employees.[44] An employer is also prohibited from fixing a camera constantly on one particular employee,[45] and the number of cameras to be used has often been limited in number by the courts.[46] The case law also suggests that once the relevant problem is solved, the employer must remove the surveillance cameras immediately.[47]

Some case law suggests that the constant surveillance of employees may constitute an unfair and unreasonable condition of employment and may be a breach of the employees' privacy right. There are exceptions in rare cases where "constant surveillance may be justified in order to deal with a massive intractable security".[48] As a general principle, monitoring should be limited to what is necessary for the intended purposes. In other words, even though an employer may have good reasons for installing a surveillance device in the workplace, the way in which this device is installed will be inadequate if it subjects employees to constant surveillance.

The principles outlined above can be transposed to surveillance by other means than cameras. In sum, employers have the right to protect their business against theft and other problems, but any surveillance

---

44 See *Re Puretex Knitting Co. Ltd. and. C.T.C.U.* (1979), 23 L.A.C. (2d) 14 (Ont. Arb. Bd.).

45 *Paquin v. Distribution Nadair Ltée.*, D.T.E. 92T-905.

46 *Liberty Smelting Works (1962) Ltd v. Syndicat international des travailleurs unis de l'automobile, de l'aéronautique et des instruments aratoires d'Amérique (TUA), local 1470*, [1972] SAG 1039.

47 *Liberty Smelting, ibid.*, at 1045.

48 *Re Puretex Knitting Co. Ltd. and C.T.C.U.* (1979), 23 L.A.C. (2d) 14 (Ont. Arb. Bd.). See also *Association des techniciennes et techniciens en diététique du Québec v. Centre hospitalier Côte-des-Neiges*, [1993] T.A. 1021. In this case, five thefts had occurred in the place of business within a six-month period, including the theft of almost $4,000 from a safe. To identify the culprits, the employer installed a video camera. However, the installation was not properly done and the technician's office was filmed instead of the safe within it. According to the arbitrator, nothing in the evidence indicated that the dignity, honour, or reputation of the employees who were filmed had been violated by the installation of the camera, or that the camera had violated their right to privacy under s. 5 of the *Quebec Charter*. Although it is true that, by virtue of s. 46 of the *Quebec Charter*, a constant surveillance of employees could constitute an unfair and unreasonable condition of employment, again, this depends on the circumstances in question. In this case, given the situation of repeated thefts, the arbitrator found it was not unreasonable for the employer to use an electronic surveillance device. However, the arbitrator also felt that the employer should have monitored the safe in a way that would have had the least impact on the rights of the employees. By installing the camera improperly, the employer failed in this regard. The arbitrator also found that even if surveillance can be used and justified to prevent theft, a constant surveillance of employees would constitute an unreasonable working condition.

carried out must be limited to what is necessary to prevent those problems without creating unjust or unreasonable working conditions.

(e) Conclusion

Existing legislation and jurisprudence regarding the exercise of electronic surveillance in the workplace reveal certain general principles applicable to the monitoring of an employee's Web access, and e-mail use and use of other technologies in the workplace. It is clear that employees have the fundamental right to the respect of their privacy and to fair and reasonable working conditions. These rights, however, are not absolute. The employer has the correlative right, by virtue of its managerial functions and the subordination of the employee to its authority, to control his employees' work, which may include monitoring the employees' use of information technology in the workplace. However, the employer does not have the *prima facie* right to have recourse to devices to monitor the behaviour and the productivity of its employees. The employer may be permitted to monitor employees in particular circumstances that warrant it, for example when the employer can show that a serious security problem exists or that acts of dishonesty such as thefts are being committed. In such a case, the employer must show that he had no other choice or means available to resolve the problem. If the employer does monitor its employees' Web access or e-mail use, there should be serious reasons for doing so, and the employer must respect the employees' right to just and reasonable working conditions. A continuous monitoring of employees could constitute an unfair and unreasonable condition of employment. A fair balance must be reached between the employees' right to privacy and the employer's right to control and manage the organization.

III. PRACTICAL SOLUTIONS AND CONSIDERATIONS: A POLICY ON WEB ACCESS AND E-MAIL USE IN THE WORKPLACE

As discussed in Section I above, employers can face many risks when employees are given computers with Web access or e-mail functionality. These include the risks of financial loss, the loss of competitive advantage and the possibility of direct or vicarious liability. In order to limit these risks, employers might chose to monitor the employees' use of technologies, but this might lead to possible violations of the employees' right to privacy.

Therefore, the question remains: in practice, how can employers limit these risks inherent to the use of workplace technologies, while at the same time ensuring that employees' privacy rights are not violated? In light of the legislative scheme and the jurisprudence context previously discussed, the following sets out some practical suggestions.

A. Adoption and Enforcement of a Policy

The most important and obvious way that an employer can address the foregoing concern is to formulate a written policy regarding the employees' use of e-mail, voice mail, computers and Web access. The policy should be as thorough as possible, preferably including the key terms discussed below. A good policy can address many of the issues that an employer faces in relation to the privacy rights of its employees. First of all, a policy that binds an employee will serve as consent to the employer's monitoring in compliance with such policy, and reduce the employee's expectation of privacy. A policy can be binding upon an employee if it is included by reference in the employment contract and made known to the employee at the time of acceptance. It may also be binding if it is clearly communicated to employees, who acknowledge having received and read the policy. In addition, the policy must be consistently enforced.

A policy may serve as proof of implied consent to the employer's monitoring if it was explicitly brought to the attention of the employee. In that case, the employer can use the policy to support the argument that the employee had a reduced expectation of privacy. In addition, once employees are informed that the employer may monitor their communications, they will hopefully limit the amount of personal use that they make of the technology, thus reducing the risk of a decrease in productivity.

A clear policy can also be useful to reduce the risk of criminal liability for the interception of a private communication under s. 184 of the *Criminal Code.*

To be effective as a means to counter expectations of privacy, the policy should respect a number of basic conditions. Obviously, the policy should not conflict with the contract of employment or the collective agreement. It has to be well publicized or properly made known to employees.[49]

---

[49] *Hadfield v. New Brunswick Electric Power Commission*, [1999] N.B.L.A.A. No. 16 (Arbitrator Bruce). The arbitrator held that the employer had not implemented a policy or instructed employees that the company e-mail system was not to be used for personal matters.

It should be reasonable, non-arbitrary, and non-ambiguous.[50] The policy should be enforced in a constant, uniform and non-discriminatory manner. For example, in a case where an employee was discharged for personal Internet use, the employer's failure to react to non-work-related Internet use contrary to the policy by other employees resulted in a ruling against the employer for the discharged employee, since the application of the policy was held to be inconsistent.[51]

The policy should specifically set out which workplace technologies might be monitored by the employer. It should also set out the sanctions to be enforced against employees in the case of a breach. More particularly, a policy specific to technology should indicate what equipment and software the employees are permitted to use, the scope of such use and to what extent they can be used for personal purposes.

The policy should also inform employees that the use of these technologies must be limited to business purposes.[52] However, in most business contexts, it would be unreasonable for an employer to expect that employees will never use these technologies for personal purposes, although the employer may sometimes justify a very strict prohibition on personal use if it would if seriously affect the business of the organization. For example, it would likely be reasonable to prohibit employees in a customer service call centre from (except in the case of an emergency) making personal calls at their work stations in order for the customer service phone lines to be kept free for clients.[53] If the employer plans to authorize or tolerate the use of the workplace technologies for personal purposes, certain key terms should be included in the written policy that provide for fair information gathering practices, as discussed below.

When enforcing its Web access and e-mail use policy, an employer must keep in mind the methodology used in monitoring the employees. Continuous monitoring of employee use could constitute an unreasonable working condition. Any monitoring, recording or storage of data should be done in the form of periodical audits or checks from time to time and should not be focused on one particular employee, except if the employer has real and serious reasons to believe that the employee has committed, is committing, or will commit a breach of his or her obligations or duties owed towards the employer. For example, in the context of data file

---

50 *Association des professionnels de la Régie régionale de la santé et des services sociaux 002 (CSN) et Régie regionale de la santé et des services sociaux du Saguency-Lac St. Jean* (2002), RJDT 261.

51 *Chronicle Journal and Thunder Bay Typographical Union, Local 44 (Barichello Grievance),* [2000] O.L.A.A. No. 575.

52 *Telus Communications (a Division of Telus Communications Inc.) v. Telecommunications Workers Union (Day Grievance),* [2001] C.L.A.D. No. 106.

53 *Ibid.*

monitoring, an the employer's computer system may check for files of certain unreasonable size or type (*e.g.*, .jpg picture files), instead of monitoring every single file created, sent or received by employees.

Certain procedures should also be adopted in order to protect any private or confidential information that is gathered through the monitoring of employee use of workplace technologies. The person in charge of monitoring should sign an agreement stating that he or she will not to divulge any of the information obtained. Such an obligation should subsist even after the expiration of the contract of employment. Also, provisions should be made in order to protect the confidentiality of the physical evidence obtained through the monitoring. For example, copies of recordings, printed evidence, or physical files taken from an employee's computer (*e.g.*, on CD) should be stored in a secure area with access limited to a restricted number of people. Electronic files should be kept on secure servers protected by passwords. In addition, a precise destruction dates and a secure method of destruction should be established.

B. How to Draft a Policy

1. Identify Purposes

Prior to drafting a policy, the management of the organization should take appropriate time to consider and determine the intended purpose of the policy. The needs of the organization to be fulfilled by the policy must first be identified, usually through discussions among members of management. Such needs may also be identified following comments or suggestions by personnel, suppliers, customers or by other third parties, or through discussions with legal counsel. Management should then establish the objectives that it seeks in drafting and implementing the policy.

2. Identify Persons/Entities Covered by the Policy (Scope)

Management should identify the persons, department, divisions or other economic entities that are to be covered by the scope of the policy. For example, one set of rules might apply to consultants of an organization while a different set of rules on the same issue might apply to employees.

3. Identify Responsible Individuals

The individuals responsible for the implementation of the policy and its enforcement should be identified in the policy itself. The persons to contact in case of questions on the interpretation and application of the policy should also be identified.

It is always better to identify such persons by title or position rather than by name.

4. Review Current Practices

A process of internal review should be put in place to evaluate current practices and identify their deficiencies in terms of management, practicality and legality. Any existing written policies should be identified and reviewed, since changes to these policies will have to be clearly identified and publicised. Practices that are not written but that are established within the organization must also be identified, as they may be considered as part of the current conditions of employment of the employees of the organization.

5. Consult Internally on Past Problems

An audit of problematic issues that arose in the past should also be undertaken. This may lead to a better understanding of the deficiencies of the current practices and present an opportunity to identify practical solutions to these issues.

6. Review Applicable Legal Principles

When drafting a policy, the applicable legal principles should always be kept in mind, so as to avoid conflict between the terms of the policy and these principles; this will minimize uncertainty in the application of the policy. This should also help preserve the image of the organization as a good corporate citizen.

It is advisable to consult legal counsel when dealing with policies that may affect the work conditions of employees, such as Web-use policies.

7. Drafting Principles

In terms of actual drafting, the title of the policy should be the first clear indication of its purpose. A short introductory paragraph should also be drafted to establish the intended purpose, spirit and scope of the policy. This paragraph can then serve as a basis for the interpretation of the remainder of the policy.

The policy should be drafted in a straightforward, clear and concise manner, so as to be easily understood by those governed by the policy. The use of headings and subheadings is also a useful tool in clarifying concepts used in a policy.

As much as possible, the policy should use vocabulary corresponding to the daily functions of the targeted individuals. Ambiguity should be avoided as much as possible and the use of definitions will assist in eliminating ambiguities.

The policy must indicate the date of entry into force of policy and include an update mechanism. For example, the policy could state that it comes into force on January 1, 2006 and will remain in force until updated by the posting of a new policy or new version of the policy on the organization's Intranet.

8. Implementation Mechanism and Training

The persons targeted by the policy should receive information of the scope of the policy and its content. In addition, those identified as being responsible for the administration and implementation of the policy should receive adequate training and resources to ensure that the policy is administered in a consistent, non-discriminatory manner and in compliance with the applicable legal principles and management's objectives.

C. Key Terms of the Policy

To be effective, the employer's policy must include a reference to all the important details pertinent for the employee to be able to determine the permitted uses of the technological work tools and the situations where monitoring or searches could be expected. The policy adopted by the employer should therefore refer to the issues discussed in this Section.

1. Description of Purpose

The primary purpose or purposes of the policy should be described. For example, the policy may state that it is intended to provide the rules of access and use of electronic communications tools and resources provided by the employer as well as to establish procedures (such as security procedures) to be followed by the employees in this context. The purpose of the policy is also to reduce the risks to which the employer may be exposed through the way of such tools. It also serves to inform employees of the potential consequences, including disciplinary sanctions, of failing to comply with the policy.

2. Ownership and Control of Equipment

The employer should list, in the policy, the technologies that are intended to be covered by the policy, such as e-mail, voice mail, computers, software and Internet/Web-use. The employer should remind employees that the technological tools referred to in the policy belong to the organization and form part of its assets and are to be used for business purposes. Consequently, the policy should state that it is expected that employees will make limited personal use of such technological tools, or that technological tools are not for personal use, if this is warranted in the circumstances, as outlined above.

3. Rules of Use

The policy should remind employees of certain general rules to be followed when using technological work tools, such as prudence, diligence, professionalism and respect for the rights of others. More specifically, employees should be reminded of the duty of loyalty or fidelity that they owe their employer in terms of the quality and quantity of work that is expected of them. Employees should also be reminded that they may not use any confidential information to the detriment of the company. The policy should also define the scope of what constitutes confidential information.

The policy should indicate the security procedures that each employee must follow. For example, these rules may include a reminder to employees to never disclose their password, to always log out when they are not at their desk, to get permission from the network administrator before downloading anything onto their workstation and to use the employer-approved clause demanding confidentiality in their business e-mails (usually automatically applied using an e-mail programs signature function). The policy may also include restrictions on making statements on the Internet or on group discussion boards. Mention should also be given to the fact that communications by e-mail, in chat groups, by posting items to newsgroups, on personal Web sites, on gripe sites and on Web logs ("blogs") require the exercise of care, given the ease of distributing messages electronically and the risk that the employee may be viewed as having the authority to make statements on behalf of the employer.

In addition, the policy should contain specific restrictions on the downloading and use by employees of open source software, shareware and freeware and instructions for seeking approval from the appropriate authority within the organization if any software is to be downloaded to the employee's work station.

4. Formal Prohibitions

In addition to these general rules of use, the policy should lay out certain formal prohibitions, such as prohibitions on distributing offensive materials, disclosing privileged or confidential information and disclosing or communicating personal information about other employees. As discrimination and harassment are also prohibited by law, the policy should prohibit the use of the Internet and e-mail to discriminate or harass other employees or third parties and to criticize other employees or the employer. The policy should inform employees of the fact that sending unsolicited e-mails to an individual may constitute a use of such individual's personal information, requiring the individual's consent under personal information protection legislation and that, in case of doubt, guidance should be obtained from the proper authority within the organization. The policy should mention that the employer's computer resources should never be used to infringe copyright. The employer may also wish to prohibit the use of computer games, the sending of chain mail or the sending of spam. The policy should make clear that the electronic tools provided to the employee cannot be used for any criminal activities, including hacking into the employer's computers or a third party's system or impersonating someone else.

5. Notice to Employees

Employees should be advised of the possibility that the employer will monitor their e-mail, voice mail, computer systems, Web access and work stations. In addition to the policy, the employment contract or collective agreement may also be drafted to include a specific provision to this effect. The employer's policy should clearly define the extent of the employees' private sphere of use regarding the specified technologies. For example, if e-mail is going to be accessible by the employer, the policy should expressly state it. The policy should be easily accessible to employees, it should be explained to all employees, included in the employee handbook and distributed and made available to all employees. For a discussion ensuring the enforceability of policies, please see Section III.A above.

6. Notice to Customers and Clients

The privacy concerns of the employers must also extend to the persons with whom the employee is communicating, whether such persons are customers/clients or third parties. The policy should therefore instruct employees to inform those they are in communication with, whether customers/clients or others, and that there is a possibility that their communications will be monitored by the employer in order to reduce the possibility that such parties will claim that they were having a "private communication".

7. Distinct Area for Personal Use

In most organizations, employees will, to some degree, use the technologies provided in the workplace for personal purposes. However, the monitoring of the use of these technologies by an employer should, in theory, only cover business-related uses. In practice, such a system is difficult to put in place. The fact that employees know that communications will be recorded will not necessarily deter them from making personal use of the technologies. One solution is for the policy to allow personal use of the technologies during breaks and lunches and to ensure that the employer refrains from monitoring the use of the technologies by the employees during these periods. A better solution would be to create a separate workstation reserved for personal use by employees, with a clear statement in the policy to this effect. This solution would likely better protect the rights of both the employees and the organization.

8. Reservation of Employer Rights

The policy should state that the employer reserves the right to increase the monitoring of the employees' use of new technologies where the circumstances require such an increase. For example, the policy should indicate that the occurrence of thefts or other serious security problems may lead to an increase in monitoring that might not otherwise be considered reasonable or acceptable.

9. Sanctions

The sanctions applicable to a breach of the policy should be clearly indicated in the policy itself, and the potential disciplinary measures to be taken, as well as their extent, should be specified. Such sanctions may range from, for example, the suspension or termination of access rights to the dismissal of the employee who acted in violation of the policy.

10. Language

Organizations having employees in the province of Quebec should ensure that a French version of the policy is communicated to such employees.[54] Certain federal institutions will also have to ensure that policies are available in both French and English in order to comply with the *Official Languages Act*.[55]

11. Consulting Legal Counsel

Even if a clear policy is adopted and implemented by the organization, legal counsel should nonetheless be consulted before any serious disciplinary sanction is imposed, in order to minimise the risks of liability of the organization, or before information gathered through the monitoring of an employee is used in disciplinary hearings or other proceedings so as to maximize the likelihood that this evidence will be deemed acceptable and will be used by the courts or the tribunal.

---

54 Section 4 of the *Charter of the French Language*, R.S.Q. c. C-11, states that every employee has the right to exercise his or her activities in French, and s. 41 of this Act states that an employer must draw up communications to its staff in French.

55 R.S.C. 1985, c. 31 (4th Suppl.), ss. 35-38.

2

INTRANET

I. THE RISKS

Many organizations now choose to make information available to employees and even to third party customers, suppliers or subcontractors, by putting in place an internal network, or Intranet, to which access is restricted to authorized users. Apart from the obvious commercial and practical benefits that an Intranet can bring to an enterprise, it can also make the organization's policies available to employees at all times, including updates to such policies.

However, having an Intranet can also pose some risks. A potential risk of making information available through an Intranet is that of invasion of privacy, notably through the illegitimate use employees (or others having access to the Intranet) may make of the personal information available by using this tool. In addition, as an employer often chooses to make organizational policies available online in such a manner, there is a risk of disseminating inaccurate or obsolete information (although this risk also exists when policies are available in paper form). If the Intranet is interactive, there is also a risk that users may enter, store or communicate information that is inappropriate or confidential. This could expose the employer to potential liability, such as claims of harassment or breach of confidence. Furthermore, if confidential organizational information is made available through an Intranet, there is a risk that such information may be more easily communicated to third parties, due to its electronic format.

If third parties (such as customers, subcontractors or suppliers) are given access to materials contained on the Intranet, these risks are increased, since they may not have, absent an agreement to the contrary or a fiduciary duty, the obligation to act in the best interests of the organization or to maintain the confidentiality of the information.

The fact that confidential information or strategic information can be made available to employees or third parties on an organization's Intranet can also expose the organization to a loss of trade secrets and competitive advantage. Employees and subcontractors, could potentially "steal" and use the organization's trade secrets, strategic or technical information (that would not otherwise qualify as trade secrets), solicit customers and solicit employees. These risks are most acute after the end of a relationship between an organization and its employee or sub-contractor.

Many of these risks, their legal basis and possible solutions have been addressed above in the sections dealing with the issue of providing Web access to employees. This section will more fully address the issues of confidentiality and trade secrets as they relate to the use of Intranet resources. Concerns regarding personal information will also be addressed more extensively below.[1]

II. CONFIDENTIAL INFORMATION AND TRADE SECRETS

This section provides a brief overview of the legal principles applicable to confidential information and trade secrets but is not intended to be exhaustive. It provides some background for organizations to develop their policies with respect to Intranet use, as well as their contractual relationships.

Confidential information is generally protected under a contract between the discloser and the recipient of confidential information, or if a duty of confidence exists between the parties. In order for information to be considered confidential, it must have the necessary quality of confidence and it must be imparted in circumstances that give rise to an obligation of confidence. In addition, to give rise to a breach of confidence that is actionable, there must be a misuse or unauthorized use of that information.[2]

Canadian courts have recognized the existence of three categories of information that an employee may acquire during his or her employment.[3] The following is a brief summary of the three categories and the extent of protection that the courts have afforded to each:

(1) Information which, because of its trivial character or because it is easily accessible from public sources of information, cannot be regarded as confidential by reasonable persons or by law;

(2) Information that is confidential, either because the employee is expressly told that it is confidential or because it is obviously so from its character, but which remains in the employee's memory and becomes an integral part of his skills and knowledge. Once

---

[1] See the Section III on Posting Personal Information, below.

[2] *LAC Minerals Ltd. v. International Corona Resources Ltd.*, [1989] S.C.J. No. 83, 26 C.P.R. (3d) 97.

[3] *Faccenda Chicken Limited v. Fowler*, [1986] 1 All E.R. 617; *Positron Inc. v. Desroches*, [1988] R.J.Q. 1636 (C.S.).

the employee is no longer employed by the employer, the law allows him or her to use his skills and knowledge for his or her own benefit. If the employer wants to protect the confidentiality of this information, it may do so by the use of an express contractual stipulation, within reasonable limits of time, space and scope of work, restraining the employee from competing with the employer after the termination of his or her employment; and

(3) Specific trade secrets which are so confidential that, even though they have been learned by the employee and remain in his or her memory, cannot lawfully be used for anyone's benefit except the former employer.

Employers are typically most concerned with the second and third categories of information described above. With respect to the second category, *i.e.*, information that becomes part of the skills of the employee, the employer must ensure that such information is protected through the use of a properly drafted non-competition clause. With respect to the third category of information (trade secrets), it is important for the employer to ensure that information it considers to be a trade secret is in fact treated as such by the employer and that the employee (or sub-contractor) to which such information is disclosed is aware of the trade secret nature of this information.

Employees generally have a duty of loyalty or an obligation to act in the best interests of the employer during their employment, which imposes upon the employee the obligation to maintain the confidentiality of the employer's confidential information. However, such is not necessarily the case for sub-contractors or other third parties who may be granted access to the employer's Intranet. For such parties, the law recognizes that they may also be subjected to an obligation of confidentiality towards the organization in certain circumstances, notably if a "special relationship" exists between the organization and such party, giving rise to a fiduciary obligation.[4]

It is always prudent to include specific provisions in contracts between an organization and any party to which it grants Intranet access specifying clearly that any information found on the Intranet is to be considered confidential or, as the case may be, a trade secret. The agreement should also include an obligation for the third party to maintain the confidentiality of such information.

In addition, the organization should include a notice on its Intranet to the effect that the rights in any information included on such Intranet

---

4 *LAC Minerals Ltd. v. International Corona Resources Ltd.*, [1989] S.C.J. No. 83, 26 C.P.R. (3d) 97.

are held by the organization and should be considered and treated as confidential. When granting access to other parties, the organization should also implement security measures such as a firewall and password-restricted access.

Possible remedies for breach of confidence include temporary and permanent injunctions, orders prohibiting the use of or disclosure of the information, orders for damages suffered by the owner of the confidential information or for the profits earned by the person who breached its obligation of confidence and, in certain cases, punitive damages.

A. Terms of a Confidential Information Policy

1. Enforcement and Acknowledgement

In addition to specific contractual undertakings, an organisation may wish to adopt a policy outlining the obligations of its employees and other relevant parties in relation to confidential information. This policy could stand alone or be part of a larger document, such as an employee manual.

In order to ensure that a policy is enforceable, it should be clearly communicated to all employees and other relevant parties. It is prudent to obtain a written (or other express and evidenced) acknowledgement from the individuals or representatives of the entities concerned that they have read and understood the policy and agree to comply with its terms.

2. Key Terms

Many of the issues previously addressed in the section of this book dealing with Internet use policies (Section III in chapter 1) would also apply with respect to the adoption and implementation of a policy dealing with the access to, use of and communication of confidential information of an organization; these include:

(a) Scope

The scope of the policy should be specified, including the type of information covered by such policy. A definition of confidential information and trade secrets should be included. Consideration should be given to the flexibility and breadth of the definition, to ensure it covers information in all forms and on all media.

The individuals or entities subject to the policy should also be specified.

(b) Ownership of Information

The ownership by the organization of the confidential information and of all intellectual property rights in this information should be affirmed in the policy. Guidelines as to when access and use are permitted should be included, and these guidelines should spell out clearly the identity of those who are allowed such access and use.

(c) Restrictions and Safeguards

Clear restrictions on the communication and disclosure of the information need to be included. The reasons and requirement to use adequate safeguards to protect the confidentiality of the information when it is communicated, by the use of technological, administrative or management measures, should also be detailed. For example, the policy may state that each electronic communication containing confidential information must use a minimum standard of encryption and contain appropriate notices, in particular with respect to the fact that the message contains confidential information of the organization and that it is intended to be communicated to the named addressee of the message only. The notice should also require any other recipient to destroy or delete the information if received in error and to advise the organization immediately of the miscommunication.

If the right to reproduce the information in whole or in part is granted, the policy should state that any copyright or other intellectual property rights notices should be retained and that clear reference to the source of the information should be made.

(d) Third Party Information

The policy should remind individuals and the representatives of other entities that some of the information made available to them may be the confidential information of third parties that the organization is under obligation to maintain confidential. The policy should reflect such third party obligations in order to minimize the risk of liability for the organization for breach of the same. For example, some agreements with third parties may expressly impose on the organization the obligation to enter into confidentiality agreements with the organization's employees and subcontractors.

(e) Sanctions

Possible sanctions for violations of the policy should be specified, including any disciplinary sanctions against employees or possible recourses against other parties. The sanctions need to be realistic and must be followed in case where a breach of the policy occurs; failure to do so may result in an eventual unenforceability of the policy or parts thereof at law.

B. Language Issues

For organizations having employees in the Province of Quebec, it is important to note that s. 4 of Quebec's *Charter of the French Language*[5] states that "workers have the right to carry on their activities in French". In addition, s. 41 provides that every employer shall draft its written communications to its staff in French. Consequently, if the Intranet is used by an employer as a means of communication to its staff located in Quebec, the employer should adopt a practice of making all such communications available in French. This practice is especially advisable for any enterprise that is subject to the requirement to obtain a francisation certificate under the *Charter of the French Language.*[6] This requirement of the *Charter of the French Language* does not apply in respect of employees located outside the Province of Quebec.

III. POSTING PERSONAL INFORMATION

A. The Risks

When an organization makes information available on an Intranet or to third parties through the Internet, the potential risk of disclosure of personal information in contravention of applicable legislation arises.

---

5 R.S.Q. c. C-11.

6 Enterprises doing business in Quebec which have more than fifty (50) employees have an obligation to obtain a "francization certificate", according to criteria and conditions set out by the Office québécois de la langue française.

B. The Legislative Context

1. Federal Legislation and the Protection of Personal Information

To respond to growing concerns about privacy rights, in 2001 the federal government enacted the *Personal Information Protection and Electronic Documents Act*[7] to better protect the right to privacy of Canadian citizens. *PIPEDA* protects personal information (defined as information about an identified individual, but not including the name, title or business address or telephone number of an employee)[8] collected, used or disclosed by an organization in the course of commercial activities.[9] This Act applies to the private sector; it protects personal information about an individual that is held by businesses, associations, partnerships, and trade unions, while the government itself is bound by separate legislation. The Privacy Commissioner of Canada is responsible for the enforcement of the *PIPEDA*. The Commissioner plays the role of ombudsman and can receive complaints, conduct investigations and issue reports on his or her findings. *PIPEDA* establishes general principles to protect personal information. These general principles include the notion that an organization must be accountable for the information it collects. An organization must also identify the purposes for which it collects information, and it must limit the collection, use and disclosure of such information to reasonable purposes. Except in specific circumstances identified in *PIPEDA*, the knowledge and consent of individuals must be obtained when personal information is collected, used or disclosed. Organizations are also required to ensure that personal information is accurate, that appropriate security safeguards are in place and that, where it is stored, an individual can have access to their own personal information.

PIPEDA applies to federal undertakings and can also apply to personal information collected, used or disclosed by an organization in the course of commercial activities conducted within the borders of a province. Since *PIPEDA* is federal legislation, if a province wishes to avoid the applicability of *PIPEDA*, it may enact substantially similar legislation that will govern commercial activities occurring within that province, pursuant to s. 26(2) of *PIPEDA*, effectively pre-empting *PIPEDA* in respect of activities of non-federal undertaking operating solely within the

---

7 S.C. 2000, c. 5 ("PIPEDA"). This Act, as of January 1, 2004, applies to all business collecting personal information.

8 *Ibid.*, s. 2.

9 *Ibid.*, s. 4(1)(*a*).

province. Presently, Quebec,[10] Alberta[11] and British Columbia[12] have enacted legislation that has been declared substantially similar to *PIPEDA*.[13] No other province has enacted legislation that has been declared substantially similar to *PIPEDA*.

Pursuant to s. 4(1)(b), *PIPEDA* applies to personal information of employees of an organization that the organization collects, uses or discloses in connection with the operation of a federal work, undertaking or business.[14] The Privacy Commissioner has stated that *PIPEDA* covers personal information in any form, such as opinions, evaluations, comments or disciplinary actions.[15]

If any personal information of the employee of a federal work, undertaking a business other than business contact information is to be posted on an Intranet or the Internet, the specific consent of the employee should be obtained.

We have already stated that the collection, use and disclosure of the personal information of an employee who is not employed by a federal undertaking may be regulated under provincial personal information protection legislation. It is also important to note that, where a provincially regulated company sends employee-related personal information across a provincial or international border (for example through the Internet), it will be regulated by *PIPEDA* in the context of such cross-border communication.

2. Provincial Privacy Legislation

(a) Quebec

The Province of Quebec has been a leader with respect to the protection of privacy rights. It not only enacted personal information protection legislation applying to the private sector six years before the federal government or any other province, but it also protects the right to privacy as a fundamental human right under the Quebec *Charter of Rights and*

---

10 *Act respecting the protection of personal information in the private sector*, R.S.Q. c. P-39.1.

11 *Personal Information Protection Act*, S.A. 2003, c. P-6.5 (assented December 4, 2003).

12 *Personal Information Protection Act*, S.B.C. 2003, c. 63 (assented October 23, 2003).

13 Organizations in the Province of British Columbia Exemption Order, P.C. 2004-1164, SOR/2004-0220, October 12, 2004; Organizations in the Province of Alberta Exemption Order, P.C. 2004-1163, SOR/2004-0219, October 12, 2004.

14 *PIPEDA*, S.C. 2000, c. 5, s. 4(1)(*b*).

15 Privacy Commissioner, "A Guide for Business and Organizations - Your Privacy Responsibilities", Privacy Commissioner of Canada, online: <http://www.privcom.gc.ca/information /fuide_e.pdf> (date accessed: July 7, 2004).

Freedoms.[16] Section 5 of the *Quebec Charter* specifically states that "every person has a right to respect for his private life". No one can be deprived of this right to privacy except as provided for by law and in accordance with prescribed procedure.[17] The guarantees offered by the *Quebec Charter* are relevant since, contrary to those found under the *Canadian Charter*, they extend not only to relationships involving the state, but also to private relationships, and are thus directly applicable to labour and employment relations. In this sense, an employee's right to privacy in the workplace is protected.

The *Civil Code of Quebec*[18] is another important defender of individual privacy rights. Article 3 of the C.C.Q. establishes the right to the respect of one's private life as an attribute of one's personality. It states that "every person is the holder of personality rights, such as the right to life, the right to the inviolability and integrity of his person, and the right to the respect of his name, reputation and privacy". Perhaps more importantly, arts. 35 and 36 explicitly prohibit any violation of a person's private life:

> **35.** Every person has a right to the respect of his reputation and privacy.
> No one may invade the privacy of a person without the consent of the person or his heirs unless authorised by law.
>
> **36.** The following acts, in particular, may be considered as invasions of the privacy of a person:
> (1) entering or taking anything in his dwelling;
> (2) intentionally intercepting or using his private communi cations;
> (3) appropriating or using his image or voice while he is in private premises;
> (4) keeping his private life under observation by any means;
> (5) using his name, image, likeness or voice for a purpose other than the legitimate information of the public;
> (6) using his correspondence, manuscripts or other personal documents.

However, thc provisions of the *Quebec Charter* or the C.C.Q. do not define what constitutes a violation of one's private life. Article 36 C.C.Q. merely enumerates the acts susceptible of violating one's private life.As mentioned, Quebec's legislature enacted *An Act respecting the protection of personal information in the private sector*[19] in 1994, before any other

[16] R.S.Q. c. C-12 ("*Quebec Charter*").
[17] *Quebec Charter, ibid.*, s. 24.
[18] S.Q. 1991, c. 64 ("C.C.Q.").
[19] R.S.Q. c. P-39.1 ("Personal Information Act").

Canadian legislation of this kind. The Quebec *Personal Information Act* was also the first provincial legislation to be declared substantially similar to *PIPEDA*. Therefore, the collection, use and disclosure of personal information in the course of commercial activities within the Province of Quebec will be governed under by Quebec's *Personal Information Act* and not under *PIPEDA*. Unlike *PIPEDA*, the Quebec *Personal Information Act* does not exclude from its definition of "personal information", the business contact information of employees. Therefore, employee contact information should be considered personal information and its collection, use and disclosure will require the consent of the employee, unless the situation is covered by a specific legislative exception. Consequently, the posting of employee information on an Intranet or on the Internet requires the consent of the employee to such disclosure or communication. Such consent must be manifest, free and enlightened. The employee must be informed of the purposes of the communication in order to give an enlightened consent.

In addition, appropriate safety measures must be put in place to ensure that the confidentiality of the information is preserved and that no information is disclosed without the individual's consent or as allowed by law.

(b) British Columbia

British Columbia and Alberta have enacted legislation that is substantially similar to *PIPEDA*. The provincial legislation is applicable to situations where employers, in the setting of a provincial undertaking, collect, use and disclose an employee's personal information.

British Columbia's *Personal Information Protection Act*[20] includes employee information in its definition of personal information, but excludes contact information or work product information from this definition.

Under B.C.'s law, an organization may collect employee personal information without the consent of the individual if the collection is reasonable for the purposes of establishing, managing or terminating an employment relationship between the organization and the individual. The employer must notify the employee that it will be collecting employee personal information about the individual and the purposes for the collection before collecting the employee personal information without the employee's consent.

---

[20] S.B.C. 2003, c. 63.

Based on these provisions, the posting of employer business contact information on an Intranet may be done without the employee's consent. However, the posting of any additional personal information of an employee requires this person's consent, unless such posting is necessary for establishing managing or terminating an employment relationship.

(c) Alberta

Alberta's *Personal Information Protection Act*[21] also applies to personal information of employees (except in the case of non-profit organizations as defined by the legislation).

According to Alberta's *Personal Information Act*, the employer may use and disclose the personal information of an employee without the employee's consent, if; (a) the collection, use and disclosure is reasonable for the purposes for which the information is being collected; (b) the information consists only of information that is related to the employment; and (c) the employer has, before collecting, using and disclosing the information, provided the individual with reasonable notification (i) that the information is going to be collected, used and disclosed, and (ii) of the purposes for which the information is going to be collected, used and disclosed.[22] If all these conditions are fulfilled, the employee's information could be posted. Otherwise, the consent of the employee should be obtained.

C. Practical Solutions

When seeking to post employee personal information on its Intranet or on the Internet, an employer should ensure that its human resources department has adopted a clear and consistently applied policy with respect to obtaining the employee's consent for this use and disclosure of personal information and for the specific purposes contemplated, where such consent is required by applicable legislation.

The policy should ensure that the employee is notified or, if necessary, that the consent of the employee is obtained at the time of collecting the information, or at an opportune time prior to the contemplated use and disclosure of the personal information.

If subject to *PIPEDA*, the Alberta *Personal Information Act* or the British Columbia *Personal Information Act*, the employer should also ensure that: (a) it has named a privacy officer; (b) that has adopted a

---

21 S.A. 2003, c. P-6.5.

22 *Ibid.*, ss. 15, 18 and 21.

personal information protection policy which is compliance with all applicable legislation; and (c) that this policy is accessible to employees.

If subject to the Quebec *Personal Information Act*, the employer should ensure that it has informed the employee of: (a) the object of the file it is establishing on the employee; (b) the use which will be made of the information; (c) the categories of persons who will have access to it within the enterprise; (d) the place where the file will be kept; and (e) the rights of the employee to have access to his or her file and to request its rectification where appropriate.

In addition, the policy should provide that only information reasonably necessary for the purposes contemplated will be collected. The policy should also provide for a retention of information schedule in compliance with all applicable legislation, and for the safe and timely disposal of records containing personal information.

Finally, the policy should be made available in French in the Province of Quebec.

PART 2

WEB SITE ADMINISTRATION POLICIES

By having a Web site on the Internet, an organization can convey information quickly and efficiently on a broad range of topics relating to its activities, products and services. However, with increased exposure comes increased risk. To the extent that the Web site contains information that Internet users may possibly use or rely on, or to the extent that the Web site is interactive (*e.g.*, permitting users to upload information or conduct online transactions), the Web site business is opening itself up to potential liability. If the information on the Web site contains errors and Internet users who rely on such information suffer damages, the Web site business might be liable. The reputation of the Web site business may also be at risk. As well, if the Web site contains information or functions in a way that violates the laws or regulations of a particular jurisdiction, such as the safety and security of information technology assets, or individual privacy, the Web site business and its owners, directors and officers may potentially be subject to legal sanctions.

The infringement of intellectual property rights is one of the risks facing an organization if it engages in the unauthorized use of any software, content, trade-marks, processes or other subject-matter which, under local (or potentially even foreign) intellectual property laws, are subject to rights exclusive to third parties.

Web-related activities could also result in tort liability where there is a breach by one party of a duty owed to the other, which gives rise to injury. A tort may occur when content on a Web site is misrepresented and relied upon by another party to their detriment. Other torts that could occur in the Web context include libel and slander (defamation), invasion of privacy, appropriation of personality, breach of confidence, passing off, defamation, liability in conversion for misadministering domain name registrations, negligence and trespass.

Criminal liability could arise from Web-related activities in many ways. As noted above, in Canada, the interception, use or disclosure of private communications[1] could be a criminal offence. Possession, distribution or creation of content containing illegal materials, such as child pornography, hate literature or obscene material, may also result in

---

1 See *Criminal Code*, R.S.C. 1985 c. C-46, ss. 184 and 193.

criminal liability.[2] Fraud is also illegal and is becoming increasingly prevalent on the Web. Misleading or deceptive advertising on the Web or via e-mail may also be subject to the *Competition Act*, which contains both civil and criminal sanctions, or provincial consumer protection legislation.

Web site administration policies can help to minimize these risks by providing procedural guidance with respect to establishing, operating, maintaining and supporting the Web site, related information technology and services, as defined within the scope of the policy.

2 *Ibid.*, ss. 163 ff.

3

APPLICATION OF THE WEB SITE ADMINISTRATION POLICY

In drafting an appropriate Web site administration policy, one should begin by assessing whom the policy, and the responsibilities contained therein, should apply to. For example, will it apply only to the particular organization operating this Web site, or also to its parent, subsidiaries or affiliated entities? Will it apply only to the employees of the organization or also to any subcontractors, consultants, agents or other representatives? This question is relevant since in order to ensure that the Web site administration policy is enforceable against third parties, one must incorporate it into the agreements entered into with such parties. One should also ensure that the Web policy is consistent with the organization's contracting policies and procedures.

The scope of the Web site administration policy should also be clear as to the information technology to which it applies. Differences may exist between Web site administration policies for an organization's publicly accessible external Web site, as opposed to one that has restricted access or one that operates solely on an organization's Intranet.

One should also consider whether the Web policy should be separated into multiple policies to deal with each of the different aspects of Web site administration. For example, to the extent that any individuals, in particular those outside the organization, are permitted to modify or post content onto the Web site, a separate policy may be needed to deal with the review and approval process for such activities.

4

CONTENT OF THE POLICY

I. KEY PERSONNEL

In order to be effectively implemented, the Web site administration policy should list the key personnel (by title rather than by name) who are responsible for the various objectives of the policy. For example with respect to the technical operation and support issues, the organization's Webmaster may be appointed as the person to report to and who has the authority to direct modifications to the Web site. The human resources manager may have the responsibility for training and dissemination of the Web site administration policy. For content review and approval, an individual may be appointed as content manager with the requirement to liaise with the organization's legal counsel prior to the uploading of any content. For issues of interpretation and guidance, the organization's legal counsel should be consulted.

II. EFFECTIVE DATE

The Web site administration policy should also set out the date that it is effective and the date of any updates.

III. INFORMATION REVIEW PROCESS

The policy should establish a process for the identification, review and approval of information appropriate for posting to the Web site. Procedures should also be established for updating the information.

The first step in information review is the identification of a need to post particular information on the Web site. The policy may set out who will be responsible for identifying and obtaining the required information. This may vary depending upon who generates the information, who has the best knowledge of its content and who the target audience for the information is. Care should be taken to ensure that the information is not obtained in confidence or without appropriate intellectual property assignments, moral rights' waivers, clearances and licences as the case requires.

Once the information to be placed on the Web site (in particular one that is publicly accessible) has been identified and obtained, it should be properly reviewed for accuracy, completeness, consistency, non-redundancy, appropriateness, timeliness, levels of sensitivity, legal issues, compliance with privacy, securities laws and other legislative or regulatory concerns, before it is posted. It may be helpful to have the policy clearly define the purpose of the Web site, so that any approvals are consistently applied in respect of the defined purpose and general content of the Web site.

Restrictions on certain types of information that, if posted on the Web site, could expose the organization to unacceptable risk, should also be specified. For example the posting of the following types of information could be restricted:

- confidential information;
- trade secrets;
- discussions and information concerning patentable subject-matter for which patents have not yet been registered;
- technical information concerning an organization's products, services, processes, methods or operations, that can be used to a competitor's advantage;
- test and evaluation information related to the organization's products or services;
- personal information;
- defamatory material;
- sponsorships, advertisements and endorsements;
- third party owned intellectual property (including without limitation copyright works and trade-marks) and business names;
- content obtained from "free" sources such as on the Internet; and
- other information that could cause a foreseeable harm to the organization.

To assist with the identification of restricted information, the organization should implement, and ensure consistency with, other corporate policies dealing with the handling of confidential information, trade secrets, intellectual property and the protection of privacy. A good practice is for the organization to mark all documents and records that contain subject-matter requiring protection.

The policy may state that information from other sources on the Internet should not be copied but may be referenced or hyperlinked. If hyperlinking is permitted, care should be taken to ensure compliance with any online linking agreements and that no third party intellectual property (in particular trade-marks) are used in the link without the owner's permission. Furthermore, the policy should provide for the insertion of disclaimers with respect to liability for the content of third party sites to which hyperlinks may lead.

To the extent that the efficient operation of the Web site requires mirroring, caching or replicating information for performance, security or other reasons, the policy should set out a process for contacting the content owner of the information and obtaining written permission to replicate the information.

Web sites and Web-related activities generally involve the use of many forms of technology and content, such as software, hyperlinks and multimedia, which may contain multiple intellectual property rights. In Canada, copyrights and patent rights can exist in the software, processes and content that is used or displayed on Web sites and in e-commerce. As well, trade-mark rights can exist in domain names, logos, word designs or other devices (*e.g.*, sounds) used in Web sites to distinguish goods or services.

The inclusion of any copyright works, trade-marks, text, clip art, hypertext links, images and sound or video clips should be carefully reviewed with legal counsel, to ensure that all applicable intellectual property assignments, moral rights' waivers, clearances and licences have been obtained. In addition, procedures should be established to verify the source and ownership of the information.

In addition, the policy should contain a requirement for review by the organization's legal counsel of any information of a legal nature that is to be posted on the Web site, such as legal notices (including without limitation references and links to on-line terms and conditions, copyright and trade-mark notices), Web site terms of use, disclaimers and policies (including without limitation privacy, security and use of cookies). A mechanism to ensure that such review is completed in a relatively short time will go a long way to garnering continued respect for such a policy.

The policy should also provide for periodic reviews to assess compliance with established information posting procedures. Procedures for the identification, removal and appropriate archiving of outdated or superseded information should also be set out.

The above procedures must address the need for trained and knowledgeable personnel, familiar with the policy governing information review, as well as the aspects of the organization's operations considered to be critical and its vulnerabilities, in order to assess the nature of the risk associated with posting specific information to the Web site. This risk assessment must also include the increased sensitivity of certain information when electronically aggregated in significant volume.

In assessing the increased sensitivity that information may assume in electronic format, it is necessary to take into account:

- the attributes of and the susceptibility of the information to data mining (by third parties);
- the form in which the information was distributed, such as press releases, press conferences, or publicly disseminated documents; and
- the likelihood that the information could directly lead to the discovery and presentment of knowledge that would otherwise be controlled or restricted.

If the overall risk resulting from posting the information is determined to be unacceptable, the information should either not be posted or be afforded appropriate security and access controls.[1]

IV. FUNCTIONALITY

The Web site administration policy should set out procedures for management oversight and functional review of the Web site, which review should occur not just upon initial set up of the Web site, but also on an on going basis.

In order to provide guidance and consistency in the structuring, creation, functionality, flow and management of the Web site, and to minimize the risks associated with having a Web presence and doing business online, some of the terms to consider outlining in the Web site administration policy include the following:

- the requirements for any registration and renewal of the Web site domain name, including who will serve as administrative and technical contacts with domain name registrars;
- the processes for entering into Web site (including without limitation related content) development, hosting (which may also include telecommunications) and maintenance and support contracts, including who will serve as administrative and technical contacts with Internet service providers (ISPs) or maintenance providers and ensure that all contractors comply with the terms of the Web site administration policy;
- the requirements for ensuring the Web site are listed with particular search engines and search engine placement services;

[1] See discussion on access controls and security below.

- the specifications for the Web site,[2] including the coding, interoperability and compatibility with any specific browser software,[3] to be applied consistently to all web pages except those requiring special access and security controls;
- the common look and feel of the Web site, including but not limited to image and design standards, colour, font, type size, graphics, media;
- the location of buttons, menus, hyperlinks, notices, legal terms, policies (see discussion on hyperlinks, below and Part 3, Web Policies and Terms of Use on Web Sites);
- the process for ensuring all hyperlinks (*i.e.*, linked sites) are appropriate and valid (see discussion on hyperlinks, below);
- the procedures for placement of approved information on the Web server;
- the functional presentment and acceptance process for legal terms (see discussion on Section VIII, below and Section III in Chapter 1);
- the procedures for the collection, storage, use and disclosure of personal information (see discussion on Cookies, Section XII and Privacy, Section XI below);
- the permitted uses and restrictions relating to automated means of collecting information, including system log files/site usage data and cookies (see discussion on Cookies, Section XII below);
- the collection of site usage data (log files) to evaluate the effectiveness of the Web site including the creation of usable statistics for management purposes, such as the most/least requested documents, type of browser software used to access the Web site, geographical territory of access, etc.;
- the establishment of log in pages and links to them, where access to the site's contents is controlled;
- the provision of notification to users when they are exiting the site;
- the process for obtaining approvals for any configuration changes made to the Web server environment;
- the granting and monitoring write-access privileges;

---

2 Technical specifications may be as developed by the Web site organization, its Web site developer or may be based upon the World Wide Web Consortium's (W3C) recommendations, for example.

3 Incorporation of non-standard or browser-specific features into Web pages should also be evaluated in light of the potential security risks and interoperability. Use of non-standard or browser specific features may exclude a portion of a Web site's intended users. This is because certain features may be capable of installing malicious programs on networks or on individual machines, if downloaded. The same danger exists when downloading any executable file, which is why many organizations have a policy in place prohibiting downloads of such files.

- the maintaining and evaluating of audit control logs;
- the gathering and analyzing of performance data;
- the development and co-ordination of acceptance testing, maintenance, and support plans;
- the procedures and methodology as part of the Web site architecture for archiving (in particular as required or restricted for evidentiary, privacy, record keeping or other legal purposes), back-up and disaster recovery, to ensure that the information will not be lost in the event that the Web server environment is corrupted, damaged, destroyed or otherwise compromised;
- the co-ordination of mirror or cache sites with other system administrators, as required;
- the implementation of security and access controls, as required (see discussion in, Section VI, Access Controls and Section IX Security, below);
- the maintenance of access lists, where appropriate;
- the incorporation of a feedback/contact mechanism for user's requests or comments.

Many of the risks faced by Web site businesses can be minimized if a Web site agreement is entered into between the Web site business and users of the Web site. However, as with other online agreements, the issues of identity and authority of the contracting party becomes important. Technical security measures, such as passwords, cryptography and digital signatures, as discussed below under Security Section IX, may need to be implemented to reduce the risks surrounding the identity and authority of the contracting party, particularly if the Web site is interactive or contains content that may have liability risks.

V. HYPERLINKING

The ability to hyperlink to sources external to the organization's Web site is a fundamental part of the World Wide Web, and can add significant value to the functionality of the Web site. The Web site administration policy should set out the procedure for the selection, approval and maintenance of hyperlinks to external Web pages. This may require the development of objective and supportable criteria or guidelines. For example:

- hyperlinks to external Web resources should support the organization's mission;
- external hyperlinks should be reviewed periodically to ensure their continued suitability;

- a process for removing the hyperlink should be applied if the content of a hyperlinked external site becomes questionable or objectionable;
- the hyperlinks should not be presented in a way that could be implied as a product endorsement or preferential treatment;
- no payments of any kind shall be accepted in exchange for a hyperlink placed on the organization's Web site;
- the hyperlinks to any third party Web sites will be to the home page only and not bypass any legal terms or disclaimers or log in screens;
- verification of compliance with applicable third party hyperlinking policies or terms must be obtained;
- hyperlinks shall not perform any other function than merely linking to the approved third party Web site (*e.g.*, only direct visitors to sites and not perform any software downloads);
- graphics, logos or trade-marks shall not be used in hyperlinks;
- the use of framing technology to connect to external Web sites requires a discussion with legal counsel, in particular concerning trade-mark and copyright issues before establishing such links;
- if any third party Web site to which a hyperlink is made contains any commercial advertisements or sponsorships, the appropriate disclaimer should be given; and
- when, where and how a disclaimer should be displayed (including without limitation positioning, timing and size) when linking to external sites.

VI. ACCESS CONTROLS

The Web site administration policy should deal with the structuring of the Web site to provide adequate security and access controls with respect to sensitive information. Depending upon the sensitivity evaluation, discussed in the Information Review Process, Section III above, the target audience for which the information is intended, and the level of risk to the organization's interests, the policy should determine and provide guidance as to the appropriate security and access controls. The Web site policy may refer to the incorporation of differing levels of security and access controls for each section of the Web site depending upon the nature of the information accessible or displayed.

Access to a Web site, a particular Web page or content can be restricted in a number of ways. For example, it can be restricted physically, using technological and security controls;[4] contractually through the use of legal terms and conditions; or a combination of both.

Some examples of physical and technical controls that one may want to include in the Web site administration policy are as follows:

- the use of firewalls;
- the use of passwords, log in codes and/or user IDs;
- human identification, either through associated biometric devices or simply by requiring the user to enter an element that is visible and interpretable only by humans, as opposed to web crawlers;
- permitting access only to users from specific locations, as determined by their computer's IP address or a registration method (that may be combined with an external authentication process);
- cookies,[5] that if enabled, allow certain users to access certain pages of the Web site; and
- the structure, sequence and organization of web pages, to control the path of entry into and progression through the site.

The physical controls may be obvious, such as those requiring user active input, or may be more discretely hidden from the view of the user with pre-programmed functionality based on the specific user's identity.

Given that the Internet is an unsecured network where user IDs and passwords can be compromised during open transmission, policies and procedures dealing with the transmission and encryption of IDs and passwords should be implemented (*e.g.*, use of secure protocols (such as secure sockets layer (SSL) protocol) between the client and server machines).

VII. PROCEDURES TO DEAL WITH JURISDICTION ISSUES

One of the primary issues arising from Web-related activities concerns jurisdiction. Given the global reach of the Internet, it is not always clear which laws of which jurisdictions (*e.g.*, countries, states or provinces) will apply. Determining the jurisdiction may be different for each of the issues that are involved. For example, the laws of one jurisdiction may apply to civil matters, such as contract or tort issues, but the laws of a different jurisdiction may apply to criminal law matters.

---

4 See discussion on Security, Section IX, below.

5 See discussion on Cookies, Section XII.

A. Constitutional Issues

Sections 91 to 95 of Canada's *Constitution Act*, 1867[6] establish the division of legislative powers between Canada's Federal and provincial jurisdictions.[7] Some of these powers are exclusive (such as those granted under ss. 91 and 92), while others are shared.

For example, the regulation of trade and commerce,[8] postal service,[9] navigation and shipping,[10] ferries between a province and another country or between two provinces,[11] currency and coinage,[12] banking,[13] interest,[14] patents,[15] copyrights[16] and Criminal Law[17] are matters of federal jurisdiction. Other matters, such telecommunications,[18] have also been found by the courts to be under federal jurisdiction.

On the other hand, s. 92 (13) of the *Constitution Act, 1867*, confers upon the provincial legislatures the power to make laws in relation to "property and civil rights in the province". It is important not to underestimate the importance of the grant of this head of power to the provinces. The bulk of cases dealing with constitutional matters have dealt with the issue of friction between the federal government asserting its jurisdiction under one of its enumerated heads of power (such as banking,[19] interest[20] or bankruptcy)[21] and the provincial government contesting that jurisdiction under the property and civil rights power. However, the formation, execution and termination of contractual obligations fall under the competence of the provinces.

---

6 *Constitution Act, 1867* (U.K.), 30 & 31 Vict., c. 3, reprinted in R.S.C. 1985, App. II, No. 5.

7 Other areas of jurisdiction are also established under ss. 96, 100, 101, 117, 129 and 132 of the *Constitution Act, 1867*.

8 Section 91(2) of the *Constitution Act, 1867*. Although many aspects related to trade and commerce may also be provincially regulated such as, for example, employment law, contract formation requirements, *etc.*

9 Section 91(5) of the *Constitution Act, 1867*.

10 Section 91(10) of the *Constitution Act, 1867*.

11 Section 91(13) of the *Constitution Act, 1867*.

12 Section 91(14) of the *Constitution Act, 1867*.

13 Section 91(15) of the *Constitution Act, 1867*.

14 Section 91(19) of the *Constitution Act, 1867*.

15 Section 91(22) of the *Constitution Act, 1867*.

16 Section 91(23) of the *Constitution Act, 1867*.

17 Section 91(27) of the *Constitution Act, 1867*.

18 *Reference Re Regulation and Control of Radio Communications*, [1931] S.C.R. 541, affd [1932] 2 D.L.R. 81 (P.C.).

19 *Bank of Toronto v. Lambe* (1887), 12 App. Cas. 575; *Alberta Bank Taxation Reference*, [1939] A.C. 117.

20 *Ontario (Attorney General) v. Barfried Enterprises Ltd.*, [1963] S.C.R. 570.

21 *Husky Oil Operations v. Canada (Minister of National Revenue – M.N.R.)*, [1995] S.C.J. No. 77, [1995] 3 S.C.R. 453.

Entities doing business in Canada will be subject to either federal or provincial legislation, depending on the subject matter at hand, and may sometimes be subject to both, where the business falls under the concurrent jurisdiction of both levels of government. The same principles apply to federal enterprises, which must abide by provincial legislation in certain cases, except where the provincial law would affect a "vital part" of the federal undertaking and be inconsistent with federal law, or where it is legislation in relation to a federal head of power.

B. Choice of Forum and Governing Law

Where an organization's business activities contain elements that can be tied to two or more jurisdictions, two legal questions arise. The first concerns forum: in case of a dispute, which court or courts (there can be multiple courts) are competent to hear and adjudicate the dispute? The second is the governing law: the court seized of the dispute will apply the law of what country or jurisdiction? Note that in some cases, the court that has jurisdiction over a dispute will apply a foreign law to resolve it, so that the answers to these two questions may differ.

An organization doing business over the Internet may have a preference for a certain forum and governing law for practical, legal and economic reasons. In such case, the Web site administration policy should outline the best practices for ensuring that the organization, and all activities conducted on or through its Web site, will become subject to the chosen forum and governing law. In preparing such a policy, one needs to understand the tests that a court will apply to determine applicable jurisdiction for forum and governing law, and structure the organization's business activities in order to meet those tests. It should be noted, however, that these tests are generally applicable in Canada and different tests may be applied in other jurisdictions.

1. Jurisdiction of Forum

(a) Common Law

The common law basis for jurisdiction of forum or court rests on three circumstances. A court may exert jurisdiction on a defendant if:

(1) the defendant consents to the exercise of jurisdiction of that forum;
(2) if the defendant is present in the forum; or

(3) if there is a real and substantial connection between the party or the subject matter of the actin and the forum.[22]

(i) Consent to Forum

The consent of a defendant to the jurisdiction of the court need not be express, the mere fact of defending the action in court and failing to contest the jurisdiction of the proceedings is sufficient to grant jurisdiction to the court that was seized with the action. Likewise, bringing a counterclaim against the plaintiff will ground jurisdiction against the defendant in the principal action, just as the main claim by the plaintiff will be sufficient to ground jurisdiction for any counterclaim by the defendant. The most frequent case occurs where the consent to jurisdiction is obtained from the parties prior to the action, and in fact, prior to the dispute, by virtue of an exclusive choice of jurisdiction clause. (See discussion regarding choice of jurisdiction clauses in Section 2 below).

(ii) Presence in Forum

The common law rule regarding the presence of the defendant in the forum is interpreted to mean that the defendant is present in the jurisdiction for the formal service of the originating process. If the defendant resides in and does business from the same jurisdiction, the basis for this jurisdiction and the service are straightforward. Difficulties arise where the defendant resides in one jurisdiction but does business from another jurisdiction. This is frequently the case with Web-based businesses and transactions.

In the case where the defendant is a corporation, the rules vary from province to province, but generally, it is sufficient for a company to be subject to the jurisdiction of the forum in a particular province where it has an office or carries on business. It is not necessary that the head office be located in the jurisdiction. In addition, if a Web site is created or maintained in the jurisdiction, that fact may be used by the courts in analysing the question of jurisdiction. However, the location of the Web site is often just one of many factors taken into account in determining jurisdiction.[23] One key factor that the courts and administrative bodies

---

[22] *Morguard Investments Ltd. v. De Savoye*, [1990] S.C.J. No. 135, [1990] 3 S.C.R. 1077. Many subsequent Canadian cases have endorsed this test.

[23] See *Telebyte Inc. v. Kend Aid Inc.*, 56 U.S.P.Q. 2d 1150 (E.D.N.Y. 2000); *Citigroup Inc. v. City Holding Co.*, 97 F. Suppl 2d 549 (S.D.N.Y. 2000); *National Football League v. Miller*, WL 35566 (S.N.N.Y. 2000); see also *World Stock Exchange, Alberta Securities Commission, 15 February 2000 and Pro-C Ltd. v. Computer City Inc.*, [2000] O.J. No. 2823, 7 C.P.R. (4th) 193 (S.C.J.), revd [2001] O.J. No. 3600, 55 O.R. (3d) 577 (C.A.) which held that the physical location of Web site servers is not dispositive in determining questions of jurisdiction.

have used in resolving jurisdictional questions is whether the activity on the Web site is targeted to the jurisdiction in which the issue arises. The functionality of the Web site, including whether or not it is interactive with the residents of the applicable jurisdiction or used to conduct business with such residents, could have the effect of subjecting the Web site organization to the particular jurisdiction.[24] In addition, any purposeful activity directed to the development of a market for goods or services in the jurisdiction, combined with the fact that there is a Web site, even if it is a foreign Web site, accessible by persons in that jurisdiction, might be considered to have a real and substantial connection with a Canadian jurisdiction. Therefore, in structuring a Web site and preparing a Web site administration policy, one needs to consider:

(1) the location of the organization with the Web site or business (*i.e.*, whether the presence of or the activities conducted on the Web site, constitute doing business in a particular jurisdiction and therefore subjecting the organization to that jurisdiction's forum);
(2) the location of the Web site itself, *i.e.*, the location of the Web server hosting the Web site; and
(3) the location of the users accessing the Web site and whether there should be specific controls on accessibility, in order for the organization to ensure it will be subject only to the jurisdiction of its preferred forum.

(iii) Real and Substantial Connection

A court may also assert jurisdiction where there is a real and substantial connection between the parties. Many of the rules of service for the various common law provinces give non-exhaustive definitions of what constitutes a real and substantial connection. For example, the Ontario *Rules of Civil Procedure* provide for service outside of Ontario, without leave where, inter alia, a contract was signed in Ontario, the parties have agreed that Ontario courts should have jurisdiction, a tort has been committed in Ontario, damage has been sustained in Ontario from a tort or breach of contract caused elsewhere, or a person is ordinarily residing or carrying on a business in Ontario. This issue can become particularly problematic when business is conducted on the Web. What constitutes a real and substantial connection to a particular jurisdiction in many of the Internet cases to date is whether the commercial activity is targeted at the jurisdiction in which the claim is made. Therefore the Web site administration policy, and other corporate policies such as those governing advertising or marketing, should deal with the scope of the target users of the Web site, any products or services provided via the

---

[24] See *Braintech, Inc. v. Kostiuk*, [1999] B.C.J. No. 622, 171 D.L.R. (4th) 46 (C.A.).

Web site or other means and appropriate access controls for users from jurisdictions that the organization does not want to become subject to the forum of. As well, as discussed in Jurisdiction in Section (2) below, it would also be prudent to include a choice of forum clause in online agreements, although such choice may not be enforceable in certain cases, particularly when dealing with consumers.

(b) Quebec

The issue of jurisdiction of forum is dealt with by Book X (*i.e.*, ten) of the *Civil Code of Quebec.*[25]

The basis of jurisdiction in Quebec is the domicile of the defendant.[26] Domicile is dealt with differently for legal persons than for natural persons (*i.e.*, individuals). In the case of a natural person, a person's domicile is his or her place of principal establishment.[27] In an age where many people have many residences, the subjective aspect of the definition of domicile has become increasingly important. The domicile is the location that the person chooses to make his or her principal establishment, though the proof of this fact can be adduced using circumstantial evidence.[28] The domicile of a legal person is defined as the address of its head office.[29] Where a contract is concerned, Quebec courts have jurisdiction both when the domicile or the residence of a defendant is in Quebec, or when the defendant is a company and has an establishment in Quebec.[30]

As is the case under the common law, Quebec courts recognise their jurisdiction over defendants who consent to Quebec jurisdiction, either through a choice of venue clause or preparing a defence without contesting the jurisdiction. A Quebec court can also exert jurisdiction where certain specific types of contract are concerned, notably a consumer contract or an employment contract where the consumer or the employee has a domicile or residence in Quebec.[31] Jurisdiction also exists over insurance contracts where the insured or beneficiary resides in Quebec, the insurable interest is located in Quebec or the loss took place in Quebec.[32] The Quebec legislature has also granted its courts exclusive jurisdiction over product liability cases where the damage was suffered as

---

25 S.Q. 1991, c. 64 ("C.C.Q.").
26 Article 3134 C.C.Q.
27 Article 75 C.C.Q.
28 Article 76 C.C.Q.
29 Article 307 C.C.Q.
30 Article 3148 C.C.Q.
31 Article 3149 C.C.Q.
32 Article 3150 C.C.Q.

a result of exposure to raw materials whether processed or not, originating in Quebec.[33]

2. Jurisdiction of Governing Law

(a) Common Law

Where there is no legislative statement dictating the choice of law and where no governing law clause has been indicated by the parties, the courts first look to the intention of the parties. If it is clear from the intentions of the parties that the law of a particular jurisdiction should be applied, the courts will apply it. Where no such intention is evident or it is clear that the parties did not consider the issue, the court will apply the law of the jurisdiction that has the closest connection with the contract. In order to determine which law has the closest connection to the contract, the circumstances of the signing of the contract are considered. In particular, some of the factors considered are the location of the two parties, the location where the contract was formed, the location of any property dealt with in the contract, and the legal terminology used in the contract.[34]

Online contracts pose particular problems as the location of their formation is not clear where the parties are in different jurisdictions. The common law and the civil law deal differently with the problem of fixing a time and place for contracts formed over the Internet; this issue will be dealt with in Section VIII on contract formation.

Therefore, Web site administration policies should attempt to deal with some of these problems by:

(1) ensuring that the Web site and its functionality most closely reflect and are consistent with the intentions of the parties and result in the formation of binding contracts in the preferred jurisdiction;
(2) ensuring the Web site and its functionality most closely reflect and remain consistent with the closest (or at least some) connection to the contract, including:

    (a) by clarifying the circumstances in which online contracts are finalised;
    (b) by clarifying the location of the organization and the Internet users that it wishes to do business with;

---

[33] Articles 3151, 3129 C.C.Q.

[34] J.G. Castel & J. Walker, *Canadian Conflict Laws*, 5th ed. (Toronto Butterworths).

(c) by structuring the Web site such that the location where any online contract is formed is in the chosen jurisdiction of the organization;
(d) by co-ordinating the location of any property dealt with in any contracts formed over or via the Web site;
(e) by ensuring the proper legal terminology is used in any online terms and policies on the Web site.

It is prudent to include a choice of governing law clause in online agreements, as such a clause will be enforceable in many cases. The common law recognizes, in general, the right of the parties to a contract to choose the law governing their relationship. Where the choice of forum is indicated but the choice of law is not, in the absence of circumstances that demonstrate the intention of the parties to apply a specific law, the law of the country indicated by the choice of jurisdiction clause has typically been applied.[35]

Despite the general rule concerning the freedom of contract and the freedom of parties to specify the law governing their relationship, there are certain limitations to this freedom. The courts are reluctant to apply a choice of governing law clause where the purpose of the choice has been to set aside the mandatory provisions of the country with which the contract is most closely connected.[36] As well, consumer contracts pose specific issues, which will be examined in Part 4 of this book.

C. Civil Law (Quebec)

The issue of jurisdiction of governing law is also dealt with by Book X (*i.e.*, ten) of the *Civil Code of Quebec.*

The principles governing the jurisdiction of governing law in Quebec are substantially the same as those in the rest of Canada. A contract, or a juridical act more generally, is governed by the law expressly designated in the terms of the contract (or act).[37] Like the common law, the civil law is also concerned with parties who try to avoid the application of mandatory provisions by specifying a choice of governing law with fewer protections for one party. The civil law addresses this problem by mandating that all contract with no foreign elements remain subject to the

---

35 *Ibid.*, at 31-5.

36 *Bank of Montreal v. Snoxell*, [1982] A.J. No. 1018, 143 D.L.R. (3d) 349 (Q.B); *United Nations v. Atlantic Seaways Corp.* (1979), 99 D.L.R. (3d) 609 (F.C.A.).

37 Article 3111 C.C.Q.

mandatory provisions of the law of the country that would apply in the absence of the choice of law term.[38]

Where no law is designated, the courts look at which law has the closest connection to the contract, taking into account the nature of the contract and the attendant circumstances.[39] In determining the closest connection, the court looks at place of signature, location of the parties and substantially the same indicia as common law courts. Article 3113 of the *Civil Code of Quebec*, creates a presumption for civil law courts — the contract is presumed to be most closely connected with the law of the country where the party who is to perform the presentation, which is characteristic of the act, has his residence.[40] Alternatively, where the act is made in the ordinary course of business, the law of the location of that party's establishment is presumed to be the location most closely connected with the contract.[41] Both of these presumptions are rebuttable.[42] A Web site administration policy may help in rebutting these presumptions in ensuring that choice of law is considered and results in the formation of binding contracts in the preferred jurisdiction, and in ensuring that the Web site and its functionality reflect and remain consistent with this choice of jurisdiction.

Certain types of contracts are subject to particular rules as to the jurisdiction of governing law; this generally occurs in order to protect Quebec consumers and other parties in a weak bargaining position. For example, in a contract with a consumer, the consumer can claim any benefits stemming from the mandatory provisions of the law of his country of residence if the order was received from such country, whether or not a governing law clause was included in the agreement.[43]

Finally, the *Civil Code of Quebec* provides that any provisions of a foreign law whose application would be manifestly inconsistent with public order as understood in international relations is inapplicable.[44]

Although one cannot guarantee that one will not be subject to the courts or the governing laws of a particular jurisdiction, preparing and enforcing an organizational Web policy of practices can help to minimize the risks.

---

38 *Ibid.*

39 Article 3112 C.C.Q.

40 Article 3113 C.C.Q.

41 *Ibid.*

42 Article 2847 C.C.Q.

43 Article 3117 C.C.Q.

44 Article 3081 C.C.Q. reads as follows: "The provisions of the law of a foreign country do not apply if their application would be manifestly inconsistent with public order as understood in international relations."

VIII. CONTRACT FORMATION

Web site administration policies can help to reduce the uncertainty associated with when and where online contracts are formed. As discussed, these issues of time and place can have important implications on the resolution of issues related to the choice of applicable jurisdictions.

As outlined above, the principles regulating the formation of contracts are the jurisdiction of the provinces and territories under the property and civil rights power pursuant to s. 92(13) of the *Constitution Act, 1867*.

A. Common Law Provinces

The traditional common law of contract establishes that a valid and enforceable contract will be created if one party makes an offer, expressing a willingness to enter into a binding agreement with another party (whether this willingness is actual or apparent),[45] which offer is then unequivocally accepted by the other party.[46] Common law also requires that such a contract be supported by consideration (unless it is under seal).[47] "Consideration" is understood to mean the price paid for the promise of the other party[48] and may include money,[49] an act[50] or a promise of an act[51] to which no monetary value can be given.

An offer is a statement or conduct by the "offeror" indicating all the terms on which he or she is prepared to do business and presented to one

45 H.G. Beagle, ed., *Chitty on Contracts*, 28th ed., vol. 1 (Sweet & Maxwell: London, 1999) at 90.

46 *Ibid.*, at 100. Acceptance can be evidenced in writing, verbally, or by conduct. In the case of click-wrap agreements, the courts have held that the act of clicking an icon is conduct which sufficiently binds the customer to the vendor/service provider's offer in a manner which constitutes acceptance of such offer, provided the offeror has made a reasonable attempt to bring the terms of the agreement to the attention of the customer and/or the customer has had the opportunity to read such terms.

47 *Ibid.*, at 167. The essence of consideration is that it creates some benefit to the party promising or some negative impact, prejudice or inconvenience to the party to whom the promise is made. See *Robertson v. Robertson* (1933), 6 M.P.R. 370 at 389 (N.B.C.A.). Consideration may include some act, or promise of an act, which is incapable of being given a monetary value.

48 J. Swan, B. Reiter & N. Bala, *Contracts: Cases, Notes & Materials* (Toronto: Butterworths, 1997) at 217.

49 *Thomas v. Thomas* (1842), 2 Q.B. 851, 114 E.R. 330.

50 *Hamer v. Sidway,* 27 NE 256 (1891).

51 *Great Northern Railway Co. v. Witham* (1873), L.R. 9, C.P. 16.

or several "offerees" for acceptance.[52] An acceptance is the statement or conduct by the offeree directed to the offeror signifying that he/she wishes to form a contract on the terms contained in the offer. In practice, parties may disagree on the significance of a particular statement or act. To be effective, an acceptance must correspond to the terms of the offer without any alterations or qualifications. Any alteration or qualification in an attempted acceptance of an offer, creates a counter offer.

At common law, there are two legal principles for determining contract formation: the "instantaneous communication rule"; and the "mailbox rule". Under the "instantaneous communication rule", contracts that are formed by means of instantaneous communication are considered formed when and where the offeror receives notice of the acceptance.[53] Under the "mailbox rule", contracts that are formed by correspondence, such as traditional mail, are made at the point the offeree puts the notice of acceptance into the mail.

The decision *Brinkibon Ltd. v. Stahag Stahl*[54] stands for the proposition that there is no hard and fast rule, and that courts should judiciously determine whether to apply the instantaneous communication rule or the mailbox rule according to the facts of each case. Chatting over the Internet, which is virtually instantaneous, will probably fall under the former rule. E-mail, which can be instantaneous but may also depend on the availability of the receiving party, may be considered more analogous to regular mail and is more likely to have the mailbox rule applied to it.

B. Civil Law (Quebec)

In the province of Quebec, Book V (*i.e.*, five) of the *Civil Code of Quebec* ("C.C.Q."), entitled "Obligations", governs the law of contract, setting out the rules of offer and acceptance, and the rules determining where and when a contract has been formed.

Under civil law, the contract is formed when there has been the exchange of consents between the parties.[55] The exchange of consents is accomplished by the express or tacit manifestation of the will of a person to accept an offer to contract made to him by another person.[56] An

---

52 J. Swan, B. Reiter & N. Bala, *Contracts: Cases, Notes & Materials* (Toronto: Butterworths, 1997) at 217.

53 *Ibid.*, at 111.

54 [1982] 1 All E.R. 293 (H.L.).

55 Article 1385 C.C.Q.

56 Article 1386 C.C.Q.

acceptance is any statement or conduct whereby the offeree signifies his willingness to accept the essential elements of the proposed contract.

The rules respecting communication of acceptance differ between the two legal systems. Under Quebec's civil law system, there is no "mailbox rule" and contracts are formed under the general principle of when and where the acceptance is received by the offeror, regardless of the method of communication used, even though the parties have agreed to reserve agreement as to secondary terms.[57]

The *Act to establish a legal framework for information technology*[58] contains presumptions applicable to the receipt of technology-based documents. In particular, s. 31 creates a (rebuttable)[59] presumption of receipt of a document when it becomes accessible at the address indicated by the recipient, either to the sender or publicly, as long as the address is active at the time of sending.

The civil law does not recognise the concept of "consideration" in the same way common law does. Instead, it uses the concept of cause and object of the contract and of the obligation. Each contract must have a valid cause and object. The cause of the contract is the subjective reason for which a person enters into an agreement[60] and its object is the juridical operation envisaged by the parties.[61] A contract is formed when there is an exchange of consents.[62]

Therefore, how an organization structures its Web site and online transactions, *e.g.*, in real time or via e-mail, with terms of an offer or exchange of consents, can have implications on when and where the online contracts are formed and thus possibly influencing the jurisdiction of forum and governing law.

IX. SECURITY

Security is an essential element of Web site operation. The Web site administration policy should deal with the implementation, administration and maintenance of technical security and best practices. It is important for an organization to ensure that its Web site and the information posted on it is protected from inappropriate manipulation or disclosure. A well-detailed policy will assist an organization with managing the risks

---

[57] Article 1387 C.C.Q.
[58] R.S.Q. c. C-1.1.
[59] Article 2847 C.C.Q.
[60] Article 1410 C.C.Q.
[61] Article 1412 C.C.Q.
[62] Article 1385 C.C.Q.

associated with the operational integrity and security of the Web site, its content and the computer and network supporting the Web site.

To ensure the successful implementation of the Web site administration policy, operators of the Web server environment should be trained in technical information security best practices, or should have immediate access to appropriately trained individuals. The Web site administration policy may require the individuals involved with maintaining the security of the Web site to have certain levels of training, accredited certification and security clearance.[63]

The security requirements should be defined early in the process of establishing the Web site. The Web site administration policy should set out the process for conducting a formal risk assessment to determine the appropriate risk management approach based on: (a) the value of the information; (b) the threat to the organization's Web server environment and the information contained thereon; (c) the vulnerability of the Web server environment and the information contained thereon; and (d) the countermeasures employed by Web server environment. A security policy should be prepared for each Web server environment or multiple sites furnishing similar data on the same system infrastructure or architecture based on the results of the risk assessment.

Procedures for isolating an organization's Web servers that are externally accessed from the organization's internal network should be established. The isolation may be physical, or it may be implemented by technical means such as an approved firewall. Requirements for the proper installation of all security patches and compliance of Web servers and software with security protocols should be specified. Additional security measures may also be detailed, to ensure consistency with the risk management approach and security policy of the organization. Examples of additional measures to be considered include the following requirements:

- disable IP forwarding and avoid dual-homed servers. A dual-homed server is a server with two or more network interfaces. It can result in a security risk if user's machines on the private LAN can connect directly to the internet;
- limit functionality of Web server implementation;
- employ tools to check configuration of host;
- enable and regularly examine event logs; and

---

[63] The following literature on security and access controls may be consulted to assist with the preparation of Internet access and security controls: Carnegie Mellon University Software Engineering Institute, "Security for a Public Web Site," CMU/SEI-SIM-002, August 1997; and National Institute of Standards and Technology (NIST), "Internet Security policy: A Technical Guide".

- employ measures to ensure confidentiality, integrity and availability of the information.

An analysis of the target audiences for the Web site should also be conducted. This is also an important step in evaluating the risks of jurisdictional implications. Information requiring additional protection, such as confidential information between customers and suppliers on a Web portal, or information or Web activities that may be illegal in certain jurisdictions, should be placed on Web sites or specific Web pages with appropriate security and access controls.

All areas of exposure that may have an impact on security (including but not limited to the Web server, content, technical areas, communications and personnel) should be considered in the requirements for the Web site. The organization will have to assess cost versus risk trade-offs and assign security requirements accordingly.

The policy should set out when and how often security assessments will be conducted as well as the scope of the assessments. The policy may also include obligations relating to reporting back to senior levels of management.

Each organization of a regulated industry or government that is establishing a Web site should take special care in ensuring that it is in compliance with any applicable security regulations, directives, certification and accreditation requirements.

X. DISCLAIMERS AND USE OF LINKS

When external links to non-organizational Web sites are provided, the policy should set out a responsible key person, process and procedure for ensuring that an appropriate disclaimer is included prior to the Web site user leaving the organization's Web site via the link (see discussion on hyperlinks, Section V, above). This disclaimer may appear on the page or pages listing external links, or through an intermediate "exit notice" page generated by the server machine whenever a request is made for any site other than the organization's Web site.

In particular, the disclaimer should state that the organization does not endorse the product, service, Web site, information or organization at the destination, nor does it exercise any responsibility or control over the content contained on the destination site.

XI. PRIVACY

We have already discussed the issue of privacy in the context of our discussion on internal company policies, in Chapter 2 of Part 1 of this book. These issues will also be further discussed in Chapter 8 of Part 3 of this book in the context of online terms of use and agreements. In this section, we will focus more particularly on privacy issues as they relate to Web site administration policies.

Personal data collected about, or submitted by users, on a Web site may be subject to the federal *Personal Information Protection and Electronic Documents Act*,[64] ("*PIPEDA*") and applicable provincial or territorial privacy legislation. Organizations that operate exclusively in certain provinces which have their own provincial privacy legislation, may be exempt from *PIPEDA* where the federal government has declared that such province's legislation is "substantially similar" to *PIPEDA*. As of August 2004, only Quebec, British Columbia and Alberta have been exempted from *PIPEDA* due to their existing privacy legislation. Under *PIPEDA*, anyone who collects, stores, uses or discloses personal information about others, needs to satisfy numerous conditions. One of these conditions is obtaining the consent of the individual user for using his or her personal information for the specific purposes that have been disclosed to the user, which purposes must be reasonable. The implications of privacy legislation must be considered when structuring and administering Web sites.

If an Internet user submits information to an organization's Web site and the organization wants to be able to use or circulate such information in the future, the organization will need:

(a) the express consent from the user (in addition to other privacy requirements, see discussion below), for which the organization may also need to incorporate an assignment, license and/or waiver if the submission has intel lectual property rights;
(b) an acknowledgement that such information will not be kept confidential; and
(c) an indemnity from the user for any claims the Web site owner may suffer as a result of using such material.[65]

---

[64] S.C. 2000, c. 5, Part I.

[65] Lisa K. Abe, *Internet and e-Commerce Agreements*, 2d ed. (Markham: Butterworths LexisNexis, 2004).

Privacy rights and obligations may also exist under contract (e.g., non-disclosure agreements),[66] in common law where there is an expectation of privacy,[67] or as a result of legislative or regulatory requirements.[68]

The Web site administration policy should set out when, where and how notices of privacy policies, including the respective consents, acknowledgements, assignments, licences and indemnities, are displayed to users. Privacy policies describe how, in general, privacy and security of personal information is maintained on the Web site, and what specific information is collected, why it is collected, and how it is used. All information collected must be described in the policy and the purposes must be reasonable.

Depending upon the nature of the information being collected and the purposes for which it will be used, individuals may be required to expressly consent to the collection, use and disclosure of their personal information for the specified purposes, as set out in the privacy policy. Providing a statement such as "Please read the privacy policy" linked to the actual policy may not be satisfactory. In fact, in some cases, the use of an opt-out consent form may not be appropriate either and an opt-in will be required.[69] The process and Web site structure for obtaining required consents, collecting, storing, permitting access to and modification of and deleting personal information should be outlined in the Web site administration policy or a related company policy that deals with privacy matters. Consultation with the organization's legal counsel and co-ordination with the organization's designated privacy officer (naming a privacy officer is required under the *PIPEDA*)[70] is recommended.

In addition to the foregoing, some examples of privacy-related issues that should be considered in drafting the Web site administration policy are as follows:

---

[66] See S.C.C. decision in *Cadbury Schweppes Inc. v. FBI Foods Ltd.* (CLAMATO formula) at [1999] S.C.J. No. 6, [1999] 1 S.C.R. 142, 59 B.C.L.R. (3d) 1, 167 D.L.R. (4th) 577, 235 N.R. 30, [1999] 5 W.W.R. 751, 42 B.L.R. (2d) 159, 83 C.P.R. (3d) 289.

[67] See *Saccone v. Orr* (1981), 34 O.R. (2d) 317, 19 C.C.L.T. 37 (Co. Ct.) and *Palad v. Pantaleon* (June 14, 1989), York 266930/86 (unreported) where both cases awarded damages for invasion of privacy.

[68] See, for example, s. 184(1) of the *Criminal Code*, R.S.C. 1985, c. C-46, dealing with interception of private communications. In the U.S., the *Children's Online Privacy Protection Act*, 15 U.S.C. s. 6501 *et seq* and related Rules 16 C.F.R. Part 312, govern the collection and use of personal information requested from and provided by children under the age of 13. Also see the federal *Personal Information Protection and Electronic Documents Act*, S.C. 2000, c. 5.

[69] For example, it is generally appropriate to offer individuals an opt-in with respect to the use of their personal information used for marketing, at the time of collection of this information. Exceptions may apply to this rule, for example in the case of business contact information under *PIPEDA*.

[70] See s. 4.1 of Schedule 1 of *PIPEDA*.

- how requests for personal information will be made and how personal information will be collected on the Web site, *e.g.*, surveys using check boxes, e-mail forms or text form fields;
- the differences between collections of information from the public vs. collection of information from the organization's employees or service members in the scope of their employment;
- restrictions on the collection of information from the organization's employees or service members in the scope of their employment;
- how personal information is maintained in the organization's system of records (*e.g.*, information about the individual is capable of retrieval by name or other personal identifier);
- the location of the posting of the organization's privacy policy and the obtaining of any required consents, *e.g.*, through a well marked hyperlink or on the Web page where the information is first solicited;
- access and security controls with respect to personal information (see also discussion on Access Controls, Section VI and Security, Section IX, above);
- the requirement to ensure that the technical functionality of the collection, use, storage and disclosure of personal information on or through the organization's Web site is consistent with the organization's privacy policies;
- how requests for personal information, changes and deletions will be handled and technically implemented;
- the use of cookies or other automatic information collection mechanisms (see discussion on cookies, below).

XII. COOKIE PROCEDURES

A "cookie" is a small set of information sent by a Web server and stored as a file on a user's system (hard drive) so it can later be read back from that system. Using cookies is a convenient technique for having the client's Web browser remember some specific information. Cookies may be categorized as "session" or "persistent" cookies. "Session" cookies are temporary cookies that are used to maintain context or "state" between otherwise stateless Web transactions (*e.g.*, to maintain a "shopping basket" of goods selected during a single logical session at a site) and that are deleted at the end of the Web session in which they are created. "Persistent" cookies remain over time and can be used for a variety of purposes, including to track a user's access over time and across Web sites, or to establish user preferences.

Should they be used, a Web site's administration policy should address the use of cookies and differentiate between session and persistent cookies. For example:

- whether or not the use of session cookies is to be implemented in the functionality of the Web site and for what purposes;
- when session cookies shall expire, *e.g.*, at the end of a logical session;
- whether or not the use of persistent cookies is to be implemented in the functionality of the Web site and for what purposes;
- what data from cookies will be collected and what purposes will it be used for;
- restrictions on using data from cookies for other purposes;
- the requirement to notify Internet users of the use of cookies, in particular in the Web site's privacy policy and to obtain requisite consents;
- the criteria for implementing cookies, *e.g.*: (a) there is a compelling need to gather the data on the Web site; (b) appropriate technical procedures have been established to safeguard the data; (c) the CIO has approved use of the cookie prior to implementation of the data collection; and (d) notices (including the organization's privacy policy) clearly specify, in addition to other required information and the obtaining of requisite consents, that cookies are being used and describe the safeguards for handling the information collected from the cookies;
- the process for requests for approval to use cookies, *e.g.*, time frame for prior notice, the key person with the approval authority, the content of the request; and
- the safeguards to be used to protect the data.

5

ENFORCEMENT OF THE POLICY

An organization should also ensure it allocates appropriate resources to adequately support the Web site operations, including but not limited to funding, equipping, staffing, training, policy oversight and guidance, to ensure that the policy is effectively disseminated and enforced. To assist with educating staff about the complexities of the policy, the following measures may be taken:

- procedures for review, approval and reporting could be simplified into flow chart diagrams;
- short "to do" and "not do" lists can be developed and customized to the particular department;
- examples should be given and explanations of how to deal with particular common situations should be provided in writing.

As well, one may want to include a mechanism for feedback reporting within the policy, so that the policy can be amended to ensure it continues to have practical application and can be updated to meet current business and operational needs.

To the extent that compliance with any provisions of the policy need to be waived in a particular circumstance, the policy should set out the process and persons with authority to grant waivers on a non-delegable basis. In order to maximize the effectiveness of the policy, care should be taken to ensure that the waivers do not become routine and that the policy provides some guidance as to when a waiver may be sought and granted, *e.g.*, if the immediate implementation of the policy would adversely impact another essential organizational objective. The policy should also set out a reporting procedure for notifying senior management and keeping track of instances where such waivers have been granted.

PART 3

WEB SITE POLICIES, TERMS OF USE AND AGREEMENTS

The Internet is becoming the new global marketplace. By setting up a Web site that allows access by Internet users worldwide, a business is effectively opening up virtual locations in multiple jurisdictions. This can be a tremendously cost effective way to expand one's business into multiple markets. However, with increased exposure comes increased risk.

In order to minimize the risks, Web sites should contain legal terms and conditions that are often supplemented by cross-referenced Web policies. The Web policies provide additional details of the legal terms and guidelines for the proper use of the Web site. The Web policies discussed in this Part differ from those discussed in Part 1, in that they are intended to govern the actions of users from outside an organization rather than internal users.

6

TERMS OF POLICY

The following is a discussion of the principal terms that one should consider for including in Web policies on Web sites.

I. PURPOSE

Web policies generally begin by setting out the purposes for which they apply. The different types of Web policies are further described below.

II. ACCESS AND RESTRICTIONS

Web policies often supplement the Web site terms and conditions (or access agreement) by providing further details as to what the user may have access (*e.g.*, specific Web pages, chat rooms, bulletin boards, networks, databases, files, e-mail, *etc.*), what types of activities are permitted on the Web site and conversely, what activities are prohibited.

It is also important to have a good understanding of the applicable intellectual property statutes, such as the *Copyright Act*.[1] Any rights that are granted in a Web policy or in terms and conditions must be consistent with the rights held by the owners of the intellectual property in the Web site. Furthermore, if the organization is not the owner of the Web site or its content, but rather a licensee, the right it grants to Internet users cannot be broader than the rights held by the organization.

If the Web site is interactive such that Internet users can place content on the Web site or participate in discussion groups (such as chat rooms), one needs to consider whether corresponding licences or assignments of ownership rights and waivers of moral rights in favour of the organization, its licensees and subsequent successors and assigns, should be included in the Web policy or terms. It is also recommended that warranties and indemnities in favour of the organization be obtained from the Internet users to protect the organization from liability for the content delivered by the Internet users, as well as from failure by the Internet users to comply with the Web policy or terms and conditions.

---

1 R.S.C. 1985, c. C-42.

Web policies may cross-reference other policies that the organization expects Internet users to comply with, and the organization may want the flexibility to amend its Web policies from time to time. However, it is important to recognize that any terms that are not brought to the attention of the Internet user prior to acceptance may not be enforceable at law.

III. PROHIBITED ACTIVITIES

In drafting a Web policy that deals with access to the Web site, one should consider clearly setting out the restrictions on access in order to draw prohibited and potentially illegal activities to the attention of the user.

Although a Web site owner or host cannot, by virtue of a contract with its user, contract out of statutory or civil liability to third parties or criminal liability, the risks faced by the Web site owner or host will likely be reduced if the user is made aware of potential liabilities, if the user covenants not to engage in the activities that could create liability for the Web site owner or host and if the Web site owner or host has contractual or other legal remedies against the user for breach of the user's covenants.

The following activities are the subject of common prohibitions found in Web policies dealing with access restrictions:

- posting offensive content;
- posting defamatory, illegal or infringing content;
- posting information or advertising regarding restricted products or services, such as medications;
- posting information or advertising regarding prohibited products or activities, such as weapons, betting and wagering and pornography;
- using misleading advertising, deceptive practices, multi-level marketing and pyramid selling; and
- restricting access to certain users.

IV. MONITORING

In order to comply with any applicable legislation or regulations, to facilitate co-operation with law enforcement agencies and to ensure that users are in compliance with the Web policy, it is important that the policy permit (but not obligate) the Web site owner or host to monitor, audit, intercept and disclose the user's activities.[2] However, in some situations, it may be advisable for the Web site owner or host not to exercise too much control over the user's activities, in order to minimize the risk of contributory liability of the owner or host for the user's activities.

Consideration should also be given to including the privacy provisions discussed below. By having users acknowledge that their use of the Web site is not to be considered private and agree not to upload any private or personal information onto the Web site or send such information via the Web site, the Web site owner or host can minimize the risk of violation of the privacy rights of users and third parties.

2 Note that in Canada, interception, use or disclosure of private communications could be a criminal offence, unless consent has been obtained. See *Criminal Code*, R.S.C. 1985, c. C-46, ss. 184 and 193 and Section II of Chapter 1 of this book.

7

COMMERCIAL TERMS OF THE TRANSACTION

When dealing with sale of goods or services, additional issues arise that should be addressed within the Web policy and terms and conditions of use of a Web site.

Many provinces have enacted statutes to protect purchasers in the form of sale of goods legislation[1] and consumer protection legislation.[2] These provincial legislative provisions must also be taken into account when selling goods or services in a given province.

Sale of goods legislation applies where a buyer and a seller agree to a contract for the sale of goods. Both the buyer and the seller can be a physical person, a business, or a corporation. Contracts to sell services are not covered by such legislation. In Canada, all common law jurisdictions have enacted sale of goods legislation. Quebec does not have a sale of goods act, but the *Civil Code of Quebec* includes provisions generally similar to those found in sale of goods legislation.

Consumer protection legislation will usually apply when a business or its agents sells either goods or services to a natural person not acting in the course of carrying on a business. It is worth noting that the consumer

---

1 For Ontario, *Sale of Goods Act*, R.S.O. 1990, c. S.1; for British Columbia, *Sale of Goods Act*, R.S.B.C. 1996, c. 410; for Nova Scotia *Sale of Goods Act*, R.S.N.S. 1989, c. 408; for Alberta, *Sale of Goods Act*, R.S.A. 2000, c. S-2; for Saskatchewan, *Sale of Goods Act*, R.S.S. 1978, c. S-1; for Manitoba, *Sale of Goods Act*, C.C.S.M. c. S10; for New Brunswick, R.S.N.B. 1973, c. S-1; *Sale of Goods Act*, R.S.N.L. 1990, c. S-6; for Yukon, *Sale of Goods Act*, R.S.Y. 2002, c. 198; for the Northwest Territories & Nunavut, *Sale of Goods Act*, R.S.N.W.T. 1988, c. S-2; for Prince Edward Island, *Sale of Goods Act*, R.S.P.E.I. 1988, c. S-1; for Quebec, arts. 1708 to 1805 of the *Civil Code of Quebec* (collectively "*Sale of Goods Acts*").

2 Quebec has its own *Consumer Protection Act*, R.S.Q. c. P-40-1 and the sale of goods is also dealt with in arts 1708-1805 of the *Civil Code of Quebec*: See for Ontario, *Consumer Protection Act, 2002*, S.O. 2002, c. 30, Sch. A; for British Columbia, *Consumer Protection Act*, R.S.B.C. 1996, c. 69; for Nova Scotia *Consumer Protection Act*, R.S.N.S. 1989, c. 92; for Alberta, *Fair Trading Act*, R.S.A. 2000, c. F-2; for Saskatchewan, *Consumer Protection Act*, S.S. 1996, c. C-30.1; for Manitoba, *Consumer Protection Act*, C.C.S.M. c. C200; for New Brunswick, *Consumer Product Warranty and Liability Act*, S.N.B. 1978, c. C-18.1; for Newfoundland, *Consumer Protection Act*, R.S.N.L. 1990, c. C-31; for Yukon, *Consumers Protection Act*, R.S.Y. 2002, c. 40; for the Northwest Territories & Nunavut, *Consumer Protection Act*, R.S.N.W.T. 1988, c. C-17; for Prince Edward Island, R.S.P.E.I. 1988, c. C-19 (collectively "consumer protection legislation").

protection legislation enacted by some provinces has a very narrow scope of application while others are more extensive.

I. IDENTIFYING THE GOODS OR SERVICES

The goods or services that are the object of the transaction should be clearly identified as to quantity, quality, type and compliance with any specifications.

The characterisation of the object of the contract as being a good delivered or a service provided has consequences in terms of applicable legislation. For example, sale of goods legislation may provide for specific warranties and conditions implied is contracts involving the sale of goods but does not usually cover the provision of services.[3] Many service contracts, such as consulting contracts, may involve the production and transmission of some goods, in the form of physical reports, floppy disks containing information, or publications and advertisements. However, where the goods are merely accessory to the principal contract for services, neither the sale of goods legislation or the Civil Code provisions apply. The qualification of e-commerce contracts therefore hinges on the particular facts of each case. American jurisprudence on this issue has ruled, in the case of the supply of data processing services for example, that the contracts were for pure services, rather than for goods.[4]

II. PRICE

The price of the goods or services that are the object of the transaction, as well as any payment terms, should be set out clearly. With respect to interest payable on amounts due, the *Interest Act*[5] states that, where the

---

[3] Typical is the Ontario *Sale of Goods Act*, R.S.O. 1990, c. S.1, s. 1 which reads "goods means all chattels personal, other than things in action and money, and includes emblements, industrial growing crops, and things attached to or forming part of the land that are agreed to be severed before sale or under the contract of sale". See also the *Sale of Goods Acts* for British Columbia R.S.B.C. 1996, c. 410, s.1, "goods"; Alberta R.S.A. 2000, c. S-2, s. 1(h), "goods"; Saskatchewan R.S.S. 1978, c. S-1, s. 2(1)(h), "goods"; Manitoba C.C.S.M. c. 510, s.1, "goods"; New Brunswick R.S.N.B. 1973, c. S-1, s. 1(1), "goods"; Nova Scotia R.S.N.S. 1989, c. 408, s. 2(h), "goods"; Newfoundland R.S.N. L. 1990, c. S-6, s. 2(1)(i), "goods"; Yukon R.S.Y. 2002, c. 198, s. 1(1) "goods"; Northwest Territories R.S.N.W.T. 1988, c. S-2, s. 1(1), "goods"; Prince Edward Island R.S.P.E.I. 1988, c. S-1, s. 1(h) "goods".

[4] *Computer Servicenters Inc. v. Beacon Mfg. Co.*, 328 F. Supp. 653 (D.S.C. 1970), affd 443 F.2d 906 (4th Cir. S.C. 1971); *Liberty Financial Management Corp. v. Beneficial Data Processing Corp.*, 670 S.W. 2d 40 (Mo. Ct. App. 1984).

[5] R.S.C. 1985, c. I-15.

contract is not for a mortgage on real property or a hypothec on an immovable (*e.g.*, land or a building), if the interest rate is not expressly stated on an annual basis, the maximum interest that can be charged is 5 per cent.[6] Even having expressly stipulated a rate of interest, the annual rate cannot surpass 60 per cent (the cut-off for the criminal rate of interest in Canada).[7]

III. DELIVERY

The method and timing of delivery should be clearly stated, and the party that will assume the costs of delivery should be identified in the terms and conditions applicable to the transaction.

IV. LICENCE AGREEMENTS

If a Web site or the products or services for which transactions are conducted via the Web site contain intellectual property rights that are to be licensed to the Internet users, reference should be made to the licensing terms (*i.e.*, scope of licensed subject-matter; scope of rights; scope of licensee; whether or not the licence is exclusive, non-exclusive or sole; whether or not the licensee has the right to sublicense, transfer or assign any or all of the rights and any confidentiality obligations, *etc.*).[8] As well, the Web site Administration policy should require that all such terms be reviewed by legal counsel.

V. OFFERS

If an organization does not want to be legally bound by Internet users' submissions (*e.g.*, purchase requests), then the Web policy should specify that any terms on the Web site are not to be construed as "offers" but are merely invitations to treat, or advertising. It should also be clearly stated that any submission by an Internet user will be deemed to be an offer to purchase and not an acceptance of any terms on the Web site.

---

6 *Ibid.*, s. 4.

7 *Criminal Code,* R.S.C. 1985, c. C-46, s. 347.

8 See Lisa K. Abe, *Internet and E-commerce Agreements*, 2d ed. (Markham: Butterworths LexisNexis, 2004) "Licence Agreements".

VI. TITLE AND RISK OF LOSS

The moment at which title to goods and risk of loss is passed to a purchaser should be clearly stated.

VII. REPRESENTATIONS AND WARRANTIES

Organizations should ensure that the extent of representations and warranties they include in their terms of agreements are carefully reviewed. Common representations and warranties refer to authority, capacity and, in the context of sale of goods, title and freedom from liens, hypothecs and encumbrances.

Where a licence agreement is concerned, the standard representations and warranties are generally augmented with representations and warranties dealing specifically with the intellectual property issues raised by the licence agreement. Accordingly, one may find clauses warranting that the licensor has a proper title to the intellectual property rights assigned, specifying exclusive and non-exclusive areas of use and indemnifying the licensee for any claims arising from the use of the intellectual property.

A. In Common Law Provinces

The sale of goods legislation frequently provides for an implied warranty or condition regarding "merchantable quality" and "fitness for purpose". For example, where the goods are bought by description from a seller who deals in goods of that description, there is an implied condition that the goods sold will be of merchantable quality.[9] This will apply in the context of e-commerce since a company that does business over the Internet sells its goods by description (as the consumer cannot examine the goods until they are received and any money has been paid). An article is of merchantable quality where it is of such quality and in such condition

---

9 Ontario *Sale of Goods Act*, R.S.O. 1990, c. S.1, s. 15.2; British Columbia *Sale of goods Act*, R.S.B.C. 1996, c. 410, s. 18(b); Alberta *Sale of Goods Act*, R.S.A. 2000, c. S-2, s. 16(4), 16(5); Saskatchewan *Sale of Goods Act*, R.S.S. 1978, c. S-1, s. 16(2); Manitoba *Sale of Goods Act*, C.C.S.M. c. S12, s. 16(b); New Brunswick *Sale of Goods Act*, R.S.N.B. 1973, c. S-1, s. 15(b); Nova Scotia *Sale of Goods Act*, R.S.N.S. 1989, c. 408, s. 17(b); Newfoundland & Labrador *Sale of Goods Act*, R.S.N.L. 1990, c. S-6, s. 16(c), 16(d); Yukon *Sale of Goods Act*, R.S.Y. 2002, c. 198, s. 15(b); Northwest Territories, Nunavut *Sale of Goods Act*, R.S.N. W.T. 1988, c. S-2, s. 18(1)(b); Prince Edward Island *Sale of Goods Act*, R.S.P.E.I. 1988, c. S-1, s. 16(b).

that a reasonable person acting reasonably would, after a full examination, accept it under the circumstances in performance of his or her offer to buy the article, whether the article is bought for his/her own use or to sell again.[10]

The seller does not generally have the obligation to guarantee that goods are fit for specific purposes. This does not mean that a seller is free to falsely advertise goods as being of higher quality than they actually are, or as being suitable for purposes for which they are not.[11] However, in the absence of any representation, the seller is under no general obligation to provide goods of a certain quality.

There are two general exceptions to this rule.[12] Firstly, the seller is bound by an implied warranty that the goods sold will be suitable for the purpose the buyer has intended if the transaction meets four criteria:

(1) the buyer must make known to the seller the purpose for which the article is bought;
(2) the buyer must rely on the seller's skill or judgment in making the purchase;
(3) the goods must be of a type that it is in the course of the seller's business to supply; and
(4) the goods must not be bought under a patent or trade name.

The first three criteria are relatively straightforward. In order for the buyer to hold the seller responsible for providing goods of a certain quality, the seller should be aware for what purpose the goods are bought, in order to determine if the quality is lacking, and the seller should be sufficiently familiar with the goods to tell if the quality is insufficient. The

---

10 *Bristol Tramways & Carriage Company Ltd v. Fiat Motors Ltd.*, [1910] 2 K.B. 831 at 840-41 (C.A.).

11 In the case of advertising to consumers, this conduct may contravene consumer protection legislation. See Ontario *Consumer Protection Act, 2002,* S.O. 2002, c. 30, Sch. A, s. 14, *Business Practices Act,* R.S.O 1990, c. B.18, s. 2.1; British Columbia, *Business Practices and Consumers Protection Act*, S.B.C. 2004, c. 2; Alberta *Fair Trading Act*, R.S.A. 2000, c. F-2, s. 6(2), 6(3), 6(4); Saskatchewan *Consumer Protection Act,* S.S. 1996, c. C-30.1, s. 5; Manitoba *Business Practices Act,* C.C.S.M. c. B120, s. 2(1), 2(3); Newfoundland & Labrador *Trade Practices Act*, R.S.N.L. 1990, c. T-7, s. 5(1); Prince Edward Island *Business Practices Act,* R.S.P.E.I. 1988, c. B-7, s. 2; while other provinces do not target unfair practices by statutes, common law remedies for negligent and fraudulent misrepresentation still exist.

12 Ontario R.S.O. 1990, c. S.1, s. 15.1, 15.3; British Columbia R.S.B.C. 1996, c. 410, s. 18(a), 18(d); Alberta R.S.A. 2000, c. S-2, s.s. 16(1), 16(2), 16(6); Saskatchewan R.S.S. 1978, c. S-1, s. 16(1), 16(3); Manitoba C.C.S.M. c. 512, s. 16(a), 16(c); New Brunswick R.S.N.B. 1973, c. S-1, s. 15(a), 15(c); Nova Scotia R.S.N.S. 1989, c. 408, s. 17(a), 17(c); Newfoundland & Labrador R.S.N.L. 1990, c. S-6, s. 16(a), 16(e); Yukon R.S.Y. 2002, c. 198. s. 15(a), 15(c); Northwest Territories, Nunavut R.S.N.W.T. 1988, c. S-2, s. 18(1)(a), 18(c); Prince Edward Island R.S.P.E.I. 1988, c. S-1, s. 16(a), 16(c).

seller will not be held responsible if the buyer did not rely on the seller's representations in purchasing the goods. The final criterion reflects the jurisprudence concerning the sale of goods,[13] which attenuates the liability of the seller by noting that where the buyer knows the patent name or the trade name of the article sought and asks for it by name, the seller is justified in selling the buyer that article, regardless of whether the product is fit for the buyer's purpose.

Secondly, a particular usage of a trade may create an implied condition or warranty of "fitness of purpose". In other words, industry standards may dictate that goods be of a sufficient grade or quality.[14]

B. In Quebec

The *Civil Code of Quebec* provides for warranties in sale, lease, enterprise and services agreements. All of these must be considered, applied or waived. For example, in contracts of sale, the C.C.Q. imposes upon the seller the obligation to deliver the property[15] and to warrant the ownership[16] and the quality of the property.[17] The parties may also, in their contract, add to the obligations of legal warranty, diminish the effects of these warranties or exclude them altogether. In other words, it is generally possible for a merchant or seller to contract out of these implied warranties.[18] However, in no case may the seller exempt himself from liability for its personal fault.[19]

Consumer agreements are subject to an additional regime, under which the legal warranties may not be excluded. In addition, Quebec's *Consumer Protection Act* requires that the provider of the warranty be identified and that the address of this provider be included in the document under which a contractual warranty is provided. Therefore, if a merchant is providing an additional warranty in Quebec, its name and address must be included in the text of the warranty. The legislation does not require that such address to be located in the Province of Quebec, but does require that this address not be a post office box.

---

13 *Bristol Tramways & Carriage Company Ltd. v. Fiat Motors Ltd.*, [1910] 2 K.B. 831 (C.A.); *Manchester Liners Ltd. v. Rea Ltd.*, [1922] All E.R. Rep. 605; *Chanter v. Hopkins*, [1835-1842] All E.R. Rep. 346 (Ex. Ct.).

14 *Manchester Liners Ltd. v. Rea Ltd.*, [1922] 2 A.C. 74 (H.L.).

15 Article 1716 ff. C.C.Q.

16 Articles 1714-16, 1723 ff. C.C.Q.

17 Articles 1716, 1726 ff. C.C.Q.

18 Please note that this discussion is in the context of an agreement that is not entered into with a consumer.

19 Article 1732 C.C.Q.

Similar to the common law legislation, Quebec's *Consumer Protection Act* provides that goods sold to consumers must be fit for the purposes that goods of that kind are normally used and must be durable in normal use for a reasonable period of time.[20] As discussed above, it is not possible to exclude these legal warranties by agreement. Additional discussion on consumer protection issues may be found in Part 4 of this book.

VIII. LIMITATIONS ON LIABILITY

An organization with a Web site could incur in liability if, for example, the content of the Web site contains errors or is incomplete. Interactive Web sites, where users can upload their own content, may be used by users to upload material that infringes someone else's intellectual property rights, contains viruses or is defamatory or illegal. Hyperlinked third-party Web sites may also lead to problems, as previously discussed. Furthermore, the operation of the Web site itself may not be error free or uninterrupted, as there may be server outages or downtimes. Therefore, in drafting Web policies and legal terms, one should consider including disclaimers or exclusions and limitations on the liability of the organization for risks that are peculiar to Internet Web sites, as well as disclaimers of potential implied representations, warranties and conditions.

An exclusion clause is a provision that excludes the liability of one party for breach of contract, either in certain specific cases or in all cases. A limitation of liability clause is a provision that limits the potential liability of one party to a certain amount, either in certain cases or in all cases.

For example, a Web policy might disclaim: (a) any endorsement of or liability for content and hyperlinks; (b) implied representations, warranties and conditions, such as quality, merchantability and fitness for a particular purpose (as discussed above); (c) indirect damages or loss of profits; (d) inaccuracy, incompleteness or timeliness of the Web site; (e) the transmission of viruses or the occurrence of data corruption; and (f) damages arising as a result of the transmission, use or inability to use the Web site or circumstances over which the organization has no control.

However, it is important to note that an organization's use of a disclaimer, exclusion or limitation clause, might not always protect it from claims, such as infringement involving confusion.

---

[20] Quebec *Consumer Protection Act*, R.S.Q. c. P-40.1, ss. 37, 38.

The principle of freedom of contract ensures that exclusion clauses and limitation of liability clauses are valid at common law, but the courts have adopted strategies to attempt to protect the weaker party to a contract. First, in standard form contracts, where the clause involved is onerous or unusual, the clause must be brought to the attention of the other party before the conclusion of the contract in order for the clause to have any effect.[21] Secondly, exclusion clauses are to be interpreted strictly, as compared to the rest of the contract.[22]

In addition, exclusion clauses and limitation clauses may be restricted by local consumer protection law and cannot exclude liability for fraud, or apply to cases where negligence or misrepresentation induces a party to enter into the agreement containing the exclusion or limitation of liability clause.[23]

Although Quebec law allows the use of clauses excluding the liability of parties or limiting the liability of parties to an agreement, the use of such clauses is clearly circumscribed. A party may limit its liability for material damages, but cannot limit its liability for bodily injury or personal damages.[24] Even where material damages are concerned, a party cannot exclude his or her liability for intentional damages or gross fault.[25]

As in the common law, Quebec law stipulates that a clause of exclusion or limitation of liability is valid only if the party invoking it can prove that the other party had notice of its existence at the time the contract was formed.[26] Specific types of contracts are also subject to additional requirements for the validity of exclusion and limitation of liability clauses under Quebec law. In a contract of sale, a seller cannot exempt itself from liability for its personal fault.[27] Furthermore, professional vendors may not exclude or limit their liability for defects in the goods they sell unless they disclose all known defects.[28] In a contract for the provision of services (also known as a contract of enterprise), limitation of liability clauses and exclusion of liability clauses cannot be

---

21 *Parker v. South Eastern Railway Co.*, [1874-80] All E.R. Rep. 166 (C.A.); *Thornton v. Shoe Lane Parking Ltd.*, [1971] 1 All E.R. 686.

22 G.H.L. Fridman, *The Law of Contract*, 4th ed. (Toronto: Carswell, 1999) at 609. Although in the past, courts also used the concept of fundamental breach to set aside clauses excluding or limiting liability, some decisions of the Supreme Court of Canada eliminated the concept of fundamental breach. See *Beaufort Realities (1964) Inc. v. Chomedey Aluminium Co.* (1980), 116 D.L.R. (3d) 193 (S.C.C.); *Hunter Engineering Co. v. Syncrude Canada Ltd.*, [1989] S.C.J. No. 23, 57 D.L.R. (4th) 321.

23 Fridman, *Ibid.*

24 Article 1474 C.C.Q.

25 *Ibid.*

26 Article 1475 C.C.Q.

27 Article 1732 C.C.Q.

28 Article 1733 C.C.Q.

invoked if the party attempting to invoke the clause has bound itself to produce specific results and such results are not achieved.[29]

IX. REMEDIES

The Web policy (or related agreement, such as the Web site terms of use that refers to the policy), should also set out the remedies that the Web site owner or host has if the user is in breach of the policy. Such remedies may include suspension or termination of access rights, for example.

X. JURISDICTION

As discussed above, given that a Web site may be viewed and content downloaded by Internet users around the world, there is a risk that the organization may become subject to the laws and regulations of foreign jurisdictions. In fact, many agreements concluded over the Internet are likely to have an international component. In order to minimize the risk of having the courts determine the law governing the agreement and the relevant forum, all Web terms and conditions should specify which laws will govern and which courts the parties will bring their dispute in and the Web terms and conditions should expressly exclude the application of any conflicts of law and international treaties.

Generally, both common law provinces and the civil law province of Quebec tend to respect the freedom of contract of the parties and will honour provisions relating to choice of law and forum. Where the purpose of the clause is to evade mandatory laws in the country most closely connected with the contract, the courts may be reluctant to enforce the provision. This is particularly the case in Quebec, where the provisions of the law of a foreign country do not apply if their application would be manifestly inconsistent with public order.[30]

In addition, to establish a real and substantial connection with a particular jurisdiction, Web policies should contain statements as to where binding agreements with the organization are formed, where the Web site is physically located (*i.e.*, the server hosting the Web site) and in which jurisdiction the Web site is intended to be accessed (*e.g.*, by Canadian residents only). If there are specific jurisdictions that the organization does not want to be subjected to, it should implement technical controls,

---

[29] Article 2100 C.C.Q.

[30] Article 3081 C.C.Q.

such as requiring Internet users to input postal or area code, as a screening mechanism.

Note, however, that this does not guarantee that the Web site or the organization will not be subject to the laws and regulations of foreign jurisdictions. Foreign states or jurisdictions may still claim that their laws apply, or that their courts should hear any disputes, especially if the business has a physical presence in their jurisdiction (such as a warehouse or the server that hosts the Web site), or if it actively markets to people in their jurisdiction or allows people from their jurisdiction to access the business' Web site. This has been the position of some U.S. courts in various U.S. states.

As well, an organization might not be able to contract out of certain local laws, such as those requiring an to have a licence or permit, to pay local duties or taxes, to not import or sell a product that infringes upon a local intellectual property right (such as a patent), or to comply with other local laws or regulations in order to sell to customers in their state. An organization on the Web may still have to comply with the laws of a particular jurisdiction as any brick and mortar entity doing business in, or importing products and services to that jurisdiction and therefore it is recommended that legal advice be sought from counsel in each of the jurisdictions where there is an expectation of doing business, as any prudent exporter should do.

8

SPECIFIC POLICIES

I. INTELLECTUAL PROPERTY POLICIES

Web policies often also contain proprietary notices, such as copyright and trade-mark notices, which identify the owners of the various rights in the Web site and its content.

As discussed above, any rights or licences which are granted in a Web policy must be consistent with the rights that the owners of intellectual property rights in the Web site may have. Furthermore, if the organization is not the owner of the Web site or its content, but is a licensee, the rights granted to Internet users cannot be broader than the rights held by organization.

II. HYPERLINKING POLICIES

Hyperlinking is becoming very common on the Internet in terms of providing Internet users with quick access to other content or Web sites. One of the problems with hyperlinking however is that third parties may provide "deep links", *i.e.*, links into specific Web pages of the site, which by-pass the home page and potentially any legal terms which might otherwise be displayed on such home page. If an organization determines that it is important to have all users using the Web site agree to legal terms prior to using the site, it would also be of concern if hyperlinks from other sites could avoid such a process. Therefore, unless technical controls are implemented to prevent deep-linking, it is recommended that a Web policy set out clear instructions to anyone intending to hyperlink to the site as to which page of the Web site they should be linking to. Additional hyperlinking terms, such as those dealing with trade-mark rights, should also be considered.

Hyperlinking Web policies generally set out the terms that prohibit users from:

- downloading the contents of a Web site unless the user is visiting their site exclusively;
- displaying pages in a frame less than the entire size of display space on a browser program; and

- hyperlinking to or posting advertisements on or around the display of a web page.

The benefit of having a hyperlinking policy is that it could give the organization a cause of action if it discovers an unauthorized link to or advertisement associated with its Web site.

The hyperlinking policy generally contains: (a) a brief description of the format of permissible links, if any, *e.g.*, how it will work and if visible, whether the link will be textual (such as a highlighted or underlined word) or graphical (such as a logo or button); (b) specific pages on the linking party's Web site (*i.e.*, URL address) where the link will be displayed or what criteria is permissible to activate the link; and (c) the organization's web page address to which Internet users will be connected upon clicking on the link.

It is important to define clearly:

- where the permissible link can or cannot be displayed, such as on particular Web pages, frames, software programs or responding e-mail;
- the location and placement of the link; and
- the size or prominence of the link, as it appears to users and/or relative to other links.

Consideration should also be given as to whether the link will be displayed exclusively or along with other links that could potentially be competitors of the organization.

The implementation of a hyperlink by another party will likely require some software or programming. The organization may want to consider including, in the hyperlinking policy, specifications with respect to link programming, its operation or performance.

The hyperlinking policy should address whether the linking party is permitted to modify the linking party's Web site or the appearance of link. An organization may have specific concerns such as: (a) the type of content or other advertising displayed on or linked to the organization's Web site; or (b) the order or positioning of Web pages on the Web site, which could affect the impact or visibility of the link.

If the hyperlinking policy permits the linking party to make modifications to the appearance of link, either upon the linking party's request or otherwise, the linking policy should specify clearly what restrictions the linking party would have in performing such modifications. Such restrictions should include the fact that the overall look of the link will either stay the same, or be as requested or approved by the organization. However, the linking party may want, as a minimum, to be granted the right to make minor editorial or format changes to the link without the organization's prior consent. In such case, the organization would want to ensure that such modifications do not adversely affect the appearance of the link to Internet users. If the hyperlink or any modifications contain any intellectual property, such as trade-marks or logos, the hyperlinking policy should deal with its ownership and licensing, should ensure sufficient quality controls by the trade-mark owner and should also include an enurement clause, as commonly found in trade-mark licences to ensure the trade-mark owner's rights in the trade-marks are not diluted.

The hyperlinking policy should also address the procedure to provide or request changes to the link.

As with other commercial agreements, a hyperlinking policy should contain or clearly cross-reference legal terms such as the term of the permitted linking arrangement, any representations, warranties, indemnities, disclaimers, limitations on liability and governing law clauses.

III. PRIVACY POLICIES

We have already discussed the issue of privacy in Part 1 (Chapter 2) of this book, in the context of our discussion on internal company policies, and in Part 2 (Chapter 4, Section XI) where we focused more particularly on privacy issues as they relate to Web site administration policies. In this section, these issues will be discussed in the context of online terms of use and agreements.

Privacy policies and statements often exist as supplemental terms to Web site terms.

PIPEDA[1] and provincial personal information protection legislation require an organization to identify in writing, and that the individual consent to, the specific purposes for which personal information is being collected, stored, used and disclosed, at or before the time that such information is collected. The collection, retention, use and disclosure of personal information must be limited to what is necessary for the purposes identified. This would include the purposes for which any third parties (including affiliates) to whom personal information will be disclosed will use, store or disclose that information. If the purposes set out in the privacy policy are too vague, they might not be specific enough to comply with *PIPEDA* and other personal information protection legislation.

---

1 *Personal Information Protection and Electronic Documents Act*, S.C. 2000, c. 5 ("PIPEDA").

As well, the legislation applicable in Canada requires that parties collecting, using or storing personal information have in place the following procedures, which are generally outlined in a privacy policy.

The privacy policy must describe the procedures for the collection, use, retention and destruction of personal information. Note that personal information that is no longer required for the purposes identified must be properly destroyed.

Personal information should be defined. It may include, but not be limited to, names, e-mail or postal addresses, or telephone numbers, that can be used to identify an individual.

Personal information must be kept accurate, complete and up-to-date. The privacy policy must describe how the organization intends to ensure accuracy, completeness and up-to-dateness of information.

Every recipient of personal information must employ security safeguards such as appropriate firewall, encryption, and access security measures, to protect the personal information. Security safeguards must also extend to the disposal of personal information.

Individuals have the right to be informed (within a time period outlined in the relevant legislation, usually thirty days) after providing a written request, as to the use and disclosure of their personal information. The procedure for submitting such request to a recipient of personal information and having access to one's personal information, should be specified in the privacy policy as well as the procedures for correcting and deleting their personal information.

Privacy policies and procedures must be also made available to individuals.[2]

In order to comply with Quebec law, an organization must inform the individual, at the time it establishes a file containing the personal information of this individual, of: (a) the purpose of the file; (b) the place where the file will be kept; (c) the persons who will have access to the file and (d) the right of the individual to have access to his or her file and to request the correction of inaccurate information. This information should be included in the privacy policy.

Businesses should appoint a designated individual responsible for compliance with *PIPEDA*. Staff should be trained about privacy policies, procedures and confidentiality obligations. It is also recommended that organizations ensure that the third parties to whom they disclose personal information have comparable policies and protections in place. Under the

---

2 Quebec's personal information protection legislation does not specifically require an organization to have a privacy policy.

PIPEDA, the organization collecting personal information is responsible for information in its possession, including information that has been transferred to a third party. Businesses should, by contract or otherwise, ensure that any third party receiving the personal information uses the information only as authorized. The authorized purposes should be restricted to those for which consent was obtained. Further disclosure should be prohibited, unless consent is obtained.

To be enforceable and in compliance with *PIPEDA* and substantially similar legislation, privacy policies should:

- not be separate documents or hidden in footnotes or Web pages that are not immediately displayed to users at or before the time that their personal information is collected;
- be expressly consented to by users, and not merely presented to them; and
- not be unilaterally modifiable.

Note that personal information protection legislation requires an individual's consent to the collection, use and disclosure of his or her personal information, and it is not clear if merely posting a consent in a Web policy which deems access to the site as equivalent to consent is enforceable. It is therefore recommended that, where a personal information is collected through Web site, consents be expressly obtained from Internet users by means of a more active acceptance procedure, such as clicking on a button or typing in "I consent". To be in compliance with the legislation, the Web policy should also refer to a method for Internet users to access, correct and delete their personal information.

The Privacy Commissioner of Canada has released an e-kit to help businesses comply with *PIPEDA*, which kit includes, among other things, a set of compliance tools and resources.[3]

---

[3] This e-kit may be found online: <http://www.privcom.gc.ca/ekit/ekit_e.asp>.

9

ENFORCEABILITY

In order to ensure the enforceability of Web policies, it is important that they form part of an enforceable contract between the parties; this can be achieved by incorporating the policies into the terms of an agreement or by cross-referencing them in an agreement. The enforceability of on-line agreements and Web policies is dependent upon the contracting parties having had the opportunity to review the terms of such agreements and policies before accepting them and there having been an exchange of consideration or consents.

I. CLICK-WRAP AGREEMENTS

Click-wrap agreements have generally been held to be legally enforceable in both the United States and in Canada. Click-wrap agreements, requiring an act by the consumer to demonstrate his or her assent to the licence, have been considered similar to traditional, written contracts, notwithstanding their electronic format.

The enforceability of shrink-wrap agreements, on the other hand, has not been so clearly recognised. In fact, the Court of Quebec, in *Aspencer1.com Inc. v. PaySystems Corporation,*[1] recently held that the mere use of a Web site on which a notice had been posted, advising users of amendments to the contractual terms also posted on the Web site, would not be considered as tacit consent to the amendment. In this case, testimonial evidence was presented that the user did not in fact take notice of the amendments. This decision has been the object of discussions and has come under criticism by various legal practitioners in the field of information technology. It will be interesting to examine how other courts will treat this decision in the future.

The enforceability of click-wrap contracts was formally addressed in Canada in the 1999 Ontario Superior Court case *Rudder v. Microsoft Corp.*[2] This case examined the validity of a choice of forum clause in the context of a click-wrap agreement. The agreement in this case was a membership agreement with the Microsoft Network ("MSN"). Potential members of MSN were required to electronically execute this agreement

---

1 2005 IIJCan 6494 (January 31, 2005).

2 [1999] O.J. No. 3778 (S.C.J.).

prior to receiving the services provided by the company. The user was given the choice of agreeing or not with the terms of the proposed agreement by clicking (or refusing to click) on the button reading "I Agree". The plaintiff in this case argued that the form in which the choice of forum clause was presented in the membership agreement served to obscure the nature of the clause. Only a portion of the agreement was presented on the screen at one time, due to the electronic format used and the plaintiff argued that, as a result, the terms of the agreement which were not on the screen should have been treated as "fine-print" and should have been brought specifically to the attention of the party accepting the terms.

The court came to the conclusion that the click-wrap agreement had to be "afforded the sanctity that must be given to any agreement in writing".[3] The court based its reasoning on the fact that the adhering party could view the agreement easily and without difficulty by scrolling down the screen, that the agreement therefore did not have to appear in its entirety in a single screen and that "this is not materially different from a multi-page written document which requires a party to turn the pages".[4] The court held that there was no "fine-print" as that term would be defined in a written document. The court therefore upheld the choice of forum clause and treated the click-wrap agreement as a legally enforceable contract.[5]

This decision was followed in *Kanitz v. Rogers Cable Inc.*,[6] which also confirmed the enforceability of the challenged click-wrap agreement. In that case, the click-wrap agreement contained a clause allowing the defendant to amend the agreement by giving notice of such an amendment through the company's Web site, and that the continued use by the user of the defendant's services following such notice would mean that the user accepted the agreement as amended. The defendant amended the agreement by adding an arbitration clause and posting a notice of such amendment on its Web site. The Ontario Superior Court found that this clause was valid since the arbitration clause could easily be located by anyone who wished to take the time to scroll through the document for even a cursory view of its contents, since adequate notice was given to the subscribers and since the plaintiff was bound to such changes due to the continued use of the defendant's services following the amendment.[7]

---

3 *Ibid.*, at para. 17.

4 *Ibid.*, at para. 14.

5 Similar reasoning is found in the U.S. case, *Caspi v. The Microsoft Network, L.L.C.*, 732 A.2d 528 at s. 4.4.1 (N.J. Super. Ct. App. Div. 1999).

6 [2002] O.J. No. 665 (S.C.J.).

7 Please note that the result of this case may have been different under the new *Ontario Consumer Protection Act, 2002*, S.O. 2002, c. 30, Sch. A.

It is interesting to note that American courts have also recognized the enforceability of a click-wrap agreement,[8] while at least one American court has refused to enforce a browse-wrap agreement.[9] Browse-wrap and click-wrap agreements are used to set forth contractual terms in an on-line environment. Both are considered to be standard form agreements since one party drafts the terms of the agreement without consultation or negotiation of such terms with the other party or parties (standard form contracts are discussed in greater detail in the pages that follow). The difference between a click-wrap and browse-wrap agreement is that a click-wrap agreement enables the parties to be explicit in their expression of consent by requiring the adhering party to perform some affirmative act, such as the clicking on an "I Agree" button found at the bottom of the online contract. A browse-wrap agreement on the other hand usually presents the terms of the online contract in a dialogue box and the adhering party is instructed to review these terms and is deemed to have consented to them by continuing to access or browse the Web site.

In order to maximize the enforceability of Web site policies and terms of use, organizations should ensure that the Web site administration policy detailing the functionality of presentment and acceptance of online policies and terms of use employ a click-wrap mechanism that requires users to scroll through the terms of the policy and clearly indicate their agreement by an affirmative action.

As well, the Web policies and terms of use themselves need to specify what action constitutes acceptance by the Internet user. For example, the Web policy should state that it is binding when the Internet user performs a specific action, such as proceeding to access the Web site, clicking on a button or typing certain words in a box, such as "I agree". Requiring the Internet user to type in a phrase supports the fact that they have an understanding of the applicable language in which the legal terms are displayed.

By specifying in the Web policy the acceptance procedures and when the Web policy and its terms are deemed accepted, an organization can:

- address some of the problems with determining when and where the on-line contract is formed, as referred to in Part 2 (Chapter 4, Section VII) of this book;
- demonstrate that the Internet user understood and had the intention to be legally bound; and
- ensure greater enforceability of the Web policy.

---

8 *Caspi v. The Microsoft Network, L.L.C.*, 732 A.2d 528 (N.J. Super. Ct. App. Div. 1999).

9 *Specht v. Netscape Communications Corporation*, [2002] CA2-QL 492, No. 01-7860 (2d Cir. 10/01/2002).

Given that, in Canada, the mailbox rule (as discussed above in Part 2 (Chapter 4, Section VIII) of this book) will likely apply to online contracts that are not instantaneous, the acceptance of any offer must be communicated to the offeror. By sending a clear statement to the Internet user that a Web site agreement has been successfully completed and by giving the Internet user the opportunity to print out a copy of the Web site agreement, it will likely be held to be binding.

If the Web site, the products or services displayed thereon or the business of the organization is subject to federal or provincial legislation that specifically requires certain transactions or documents to be in writing, signed or original, the applicable federal and provincial/territorial e-commerce legislation may assist with determining when an electronic version of a document or signature is deemed the equivalent of an original hardcopy version. For example, at the federal level the *Personal Information Protection and Electronic Documents Act*[10] aims to clarify the rules relating to the authenticity of electronic documents by setting out a legislative scheme by which electronic data can satisfy writing requirements under federal laws that do not expressly permit the use of electronic media.

It should be noted that *PIPEDA*'s electronic documents provisions apply only to federal laws specifically listed in either Schedule 2 or 3 of the legislation or to dealings with the government.

Part 2 of *PIPEDA* entitled "Electronic Documents," provides that where federal laws contemplate the use of paper to record or communicate information, electronic alternatives may be used.[11] The provisions of this part of *PIPEDA* allow requirements to an act be accomplished "in writing" to be fulfilled electronically and allow electronic signatures to replace written ones. This part of *PIPEDA* also provides that a requirement under a provision of a federal law for a document to be in its original form is satisfied by an electronic document,[12] as is a requirement for one or more copies of a document to be submitted.[13]

Provincial e-commerce legislation has been drafted to be "media neutral," recognising electronic communications, documents, contracts and signatures as functionally equivalent to their written or printed counterparts.[14] Such legislation is aimed at establishing that the legal effect

---

[10] *Personal Information Protection and Electronic Documents Act*, S.C. 2000, c. 5 ("PIPEDA").

[11] *Ibid.*, c 5, s. 32.

[12] *Ibid.*, s. 42.

[13] *Ibid.*, s. 47.

[14] See for example: Alberta's *Electronic Transactions Act*, S.A. 2001, c. E-5.5; British Columbia's *Electronic Transactions Act*, S.B.C. 2001, c. 10; Manitoba's *Electronic Commerce and Information, Consumer Protection Amendment and Manitoba Evidence Amendment Act*, S.M. 2000, c. 32; New Brunswick's *Electronic Transactions Commerce Act*, S.N.B. 2001, c. E-S.5; Nova Scotia's *Electronic Commerce Act*, S.N.S. 2000, c. 26;

or enforceability of a contract will not be denied simply because one or more of its elements is in electronic form.[15] Similarly, this legislation provides rules for determining when an electronic document is sent and received, but does not specifically say when and where a contract is formed or whether the mailbox rule or the instantaneous communication rule applies.

The legislation allows offers and acceptances to be communicated electronically.[16]

The legislation also generally states that a legal requirement that a contract be in writing is satisfied by an electronic contract if the contract is in a form that is capable of access and retention. For example, Ontario's *Electronic Commerce Act, 2000*[17] states that the writing requirement is satisfied if the electronic agreement is in a form that is "accessible by the other person so as to be usable for subsequent reference" and is "capable of being retained by the other person". Therefore, the Web site Administration policy should set out the structure of the Web site to ensure compliance with the accessibility and retention requirements of the relevant legislation, where a document must be in writing in order to be effective. The online Web terms should also describe how the online terms and Web policies may be accessed and retained by Internet users.

Every province, with the exception of Quebec,[18] has modelled its e-commerce legislation on the *Uniform Electronic Commerce Act* (the "*UECA*") proposed by the Uniform Law Conference of Canada ("ULCC").[19] Adopted by the ULCC on September 30, 1999, this legal model was intended to place online documents (contracts, in particular), on an equal basis with hardcopy offline documents.

Ontario's *Electronic Commerce Act, 2000*, S.O. 2000, c. 17; Prince Edward Island's *Electronic Data Transmission Act*, S.P.E.I. 1997, c. 63; Saskatchewan's *Electronic Information and Documents Act*, 2000, S.S. 2000, c. E-7.22; Newfoundland and Labrador's, *Electronic Commerce Act*, S.N.L. 2001, c. E-5.2; and the Yukon's *Electronic Commerce Act*, R.S.Y. 2002, c. 66.

15 See for example, Alberta's *Electronic Transactions Act*, S.A. 2001, c. E-5.5, s. 10.

16 See for example, *Electronic Commerce Act, 2000 (Ontario)*, S.O. 2000, c. 17, 19(1): "An offer, the acceptance of an offer or any other matter that is material to the formation or operation of a contract may be expressed, (a) by means of electronic information or an electronic document; or (b) by an act that is intended to result in electronic communication, such as, (i) touching or clicking on an appropriate icon or other place on a computer screen, or (ii) speaking."

17 *Ibid.*, s. 6.

18 *An Act to establish a legal framework for information technology*, S.Q. 2001, c. 32.

19 PIPEDA was also strongly influenced by the model legislation drafted by the ULCC.

In response to a need for a framework to deal with the increasingly frequent phenomenon of online contracts, Quebec passed *An Act to establish a legal framework for information technology*.[20] Accordingly, the *Quebec IT Act* adopts a broad definition of the term "document",[21] and allows documents to be transcribed using any media or technology, as long as it complies with the *Civil Code of Quebec*; the use of a particular medium is not required by law.[22] *The Quebec IT Act* further provides that the legal value of a document does not change solely because of the medium chosen.[23]

The parties should agree to the transmission, signing and use of electronic documents and signatures. Also, technological controls and security procedures should be agreed upon and implemented. Furthermore, access to and retention of electronic documents and a method of correcting errors should be provided to ensure integrity and reliability and to satisfy the writing requirements.

II. ELECTRONIC SIGNATURES

Certain legislation (for example the *Proceeds of Crime (Money Laundering) and Terrorist Financing Act)*[24] require the use of a signature when conducting certain transactions.

As discussed earlier, most of the legislation applicable in Canada, whether provincial or federal, in relation to electronic commerce transactions, is modelled on the *UECA* proposed by the ULCC.

The *UECA* defines an electronic signature as follows:

> "electronic signature" means information in electronic form that a person attaches to or associates with an electronic document in order to sign the document.[25]

The ULCC has commented on this definition as follows:

> The definition of "electronic signature" does not create a different legal meaning of signature in the electronic world. That is why it refers to an intention to sign, thus importing the general law on the mental state re-

---

20 R.S.Q., c. C-11 ("*Quebec IT Act*").
21 *Ibid.*, art. 3.
22 *Ibid.*, art. 2.
23 *Ibid.*, art. 5.
24 S.C. 2000, c. 4171.
25 Uniform Law Conference of Canada — Proceedings of Annual Meetings, 1999 — Winnipeg (Manitoba), *Uniform Electronic Commerce Act*, s. 1(b), online: <http://www.ulcc.ca/en/poam2/index.cfm?sec+1999&sub=1999ia> (date accessed: August 16, 2002).

> quired for validity. The definition serves two purposes. *First, it makes clear that an electronic signature is simply electronic information; it does not need to "look like" a handwritten signature, though it is possible to digitize handwriting so that it is displayed in that way. Second, it acknowledges that the electronic signature will not be "attached" to an electronic document the same way as an ink signature is to paper. The electronic signature may be "associated with" the document, by mathematical logic or otherwise. The reliability of the association will affect the validity of the signature.*[26] (Emphasis added)

A. At the Federal Level

The definition of electronic signature found in s. 31(1) *PIPEDA* reads as follows:

> electronic signature means a signature that consists of *one or more letters, characters, numbers or other symbols in digital form* incorporated in, attached to or associated with an electronic document. (Emphasis added)

B. Definitions Adopted in Various Provinces

Provincial e-commerce legislation also provides that electronic signatures can have the functional equivalence of signatures on paper.

Many Canadian jurisdictions have adopted definitions similar to that of the *UECA*, but with slight variances. For example, British Columbia enacted the following definition in its *Electronic Transactions Act*:[27]

> electronic signature means information in electronic form that a person has *created* or *adopted* in order to sign a record and that is in, attached to or associated with the record.[28] (Emphasis added)

This definition includes, in addition to the elements found in the *UECA*, the condition that a person needs to adopt or create the information that will constitute the electronic signature.[29] Other laws have similar

---

26 *Ibid.*

27 S.B.C. 2001, c. 10.

28 *Ibid.*, s. 1.

29 The same definition is found in the *Electronic Transactions Act*, S.A. 2001, c. E-5.5.

definitions, but substituting the word "document" instead of "record" at the end of the definition.[30]

In addition, under Prince Edward Island's *Electronic Commerce Act*,[31] the information comprising a signature has to possess certain additional characteristics. This information must be:

(1) uniquely linked to the signatory;
(2) capable of identifying the signatory;
(3) created using means that the signatory can maintain under his sole control; and
(4) linked to the data to which it relates in such a manner that any subsequent change of the data is detectable.

As a general rule, to fit into the definition of electronic signature under these different Acts, one must demonstrate:

(1) the intention to authenticate an electronic document (or record) — this conclusion arises from the use of the terms "in order to sign" or "signature" in the definitions;
(2) this intention to authenticate must be shown by entering some information (the *PIPEDA* specifies the type of information which may be used, while in certain other jurisdictions, the information has to be created or adopted by the signatory);
(3) the incorporation, attachment or association of this signature into a document (or record); and
(4) under the *ECA* (PEI), a unique link to the signatory and the capacity to identify the signatory.

The only province that has not adopted provisions similar to the above-mentioned *UECA* provisions, is the Province of Quebec. Although the Province of Quebec has enacted e-commerce legislation,[32] this legislation contains no specific definition of electronic signature. Section 39 of the Quebec IT Act refers to the definition of "signature" in Art. 2827 of the *C.C.Q.*, which reads as follows:

> 2827. A signature is the affixing by a person, to a writing, of his name or the distinctive mark which he regularly uses to signify his intention.

---

30 See the *Electronic Commerce and Information Act*, C.C.S.M. c-E55, s. 1(1) "electronic signature"; *Electronic Commerce Act*, S.N.S. 2000, c. 26, s. 2 "electronic signature"; *Electronic Commerce Act, 2000*, S.O. 2000, c. 17, s. 1(1) "electronic signature"; *Electronic Information and Documents Act, 2000*, S.S. 2000, c. E-7.-22, s. 3(b) "electronic signature"; *Electronic Commerce Act*, S.N.L. 2001, c. E-5.2, s. 2(c) "electronic signature"; *Electronic Commerce Act*, S.P.E.I. 2001, c. 31, s. 1(1)b) "electronic signature"; *Electronic Transactions Act*, S.N.B. 2001, c. E-5.5, s. 1.(1) "electronic signature"; *Electronic Commerce Act*, R.S.Y. 2000, c. 66, s. 1 "electronic signature".

31 S.P.E.I. 2001, c. 31 ("ECA").

32 *An Act to Establish a Legal Framework for Information Technology*, S.Q. 2001, c. 32 ("Quebec IT Act").

The French version of the C.C.Q. refers to "a" distinctive mark rather than to "the" distinctive mark that the signatory regularly uses. As well, Quebec law seems to include, in the definition of what constitutes a signature, the requirement of *regularity* in the use of that signature. In addition, this mark needs to be distinctive.

A numeric sequence, even if used only for certain specific transactions and not on a day-to-day basis, could constitute a signature under Quebec law.[33] It is unclear, however, if the use of the words "Yes" or "I Agree" would fulfil these requirements. In fact, these words would seem to lack a "distinctive" quality in relation to the signatory.

Although this element has not been clearly articulated to our knowledge in the jurisprudence or the doctrine interpreting the legislation, a valid electronic signature may require that the symbols used be personalised. This requirement would be implicit in most jurisdictions. However, this requirement is explicit in the Quebec definition (requiring a "distinctive" mark) and in PEI's *Electronic Commerce Act*[34] definition (which requires that an electronic signature be "uniquely linked" to and "capable of identifying" the signatory) of an electronic signature.

Therefore the Web site Administration policy should set out the Web site structure to ensure compliance with the signature requirements of the relevant legislation, where a document must be signed in order to be effective. As well, the online Web terms should describe how a Web document will be signed by Internet users and what will constitute the equivalent of their signature, *e.g.*, the typing of "I Agree" along with their initials into a text box.

III. FAIRNESS AND STANDARD FORM CONTRACTS

Even if a click-wrap or browse-wrap agreement has been found to be a valid form of contract, its terms may nevertheless be unenforceable if they are unfair and give an undue advantage to the drafting party. The fact that there is no opportunity for negotiation of the terms of the offer makes this concern more acute in the case of all standard form agreements including click-wrap and browse-wrap agreements.[35]

"Standard Form Contracts" in the commercial context are standard forms that customers must sign without any opportunity, or only a limited

---

33 Commentaires du ministre de la justice, tome II (Publications du Québec: Ste-Foy, 1991) at 1771.

34 S.P.E.I. 2001, c. 31.

35 S. Sigel, *et al.*, "The Validity and Enforceability of Web-Wrap Agreements and Assessing the Need for Legislation." Prepared for the Uniform Law Conference of Canada, May 1999. Available online at <http://www.law.ualberts.ca/alri/ulc/current/ewebwrap>.

opportunity to alter any of its terms.[36] The general common law of contract is based on the idea of consent between the parties and freedom of contract; the common law therefore tends to hold that the parties are bound by the terms of the agreement they execute. To mitigate the effects of this rule, the courts have decided that, where a contract is not negotiated, there must be a positive indication that the party has read and agreed to be bound by various terms of the contract.[37] The terms of standard form contracts must also be brought to the attention of the party before the contract is entered into.[38] Furthermore, where a written contract is ambiguous and open to more than one meaning, the contract is interpreted against the drafter of the standard form contract.[39]

As a general rule, the words of a written contract will be *interpreted according to their ordinary and natural sense* unless such an interpretation would result in absurdity.[40] In some limited circumstances, a custom or practice that is common in a certain trade, business, or profession may be taken by the court as impliedly included in the contract.[41]

Under Quebec law, a contract in which the essential elements were imposed or drawn up by one of the parties, on his behalf or upon his instructions and were not negotiable is known as a "contract of adhesion".[42] A click-wrap agreement, in which one party has no input into the drafting of the contract and indicates its assent only through the click of a mouse, is an example of a contract of adhesion.

Contracts of adhesion are subject to specific rules, that apply to their interpretation and affect the manner in which the party who drafted agreement may enforce its rights under the agreement. First, in the case of any ambiguity, a contract of adhesion will be interpreted in favour of the adhering party.[43] Consequently, the drafter of the agreement should be prudent when drafting such a contract so as to make it clear and precise. Second, to be enforceable against the adhering party, under Quebec law, external clauses must be expressly brought to the attention of the adhering party at the time of formation of the contract, unless the other party can

---

36 G.H.L. Fridman, *The Law of Contract*, 4th ed. (Toronto: Carswell, 1999) at 609.

37 *Thornton v. Shoe Lane Parking Ltd.*, [1971] 1 All E.R. 686; *Tilden Rent-a-Car v. Clendenning* (1978), 18 O.R. (2d) 601, 83 D.L.R. (3d) 400 (C.A.).

38 *Thornton v. Shoe Lane Parking Ltd., ibid.*

39 *McConnel v. Murphy* (1873), L.R. 5 P.C. 203; *Conley Holdings Ltd. v. Canadian Metal & Supply Co.*, [1986] S.J. No. 207, 47 Sask. R. 299 (Q.B.); *Hillis Oil & Sales Ltd. v. Wynn's Canada Ltd*, [1986] S.C.J. No. 9, [1986] 1 S.C.R. 57.

40 *Suncor Inc. v. Norcen Int. Ltd.*, [1988] A.J. No. 706, 89 A.R. 200 (Q.B.).

41 *Georgia Construction Co. v. Pacific Great Eastern Railway Co.*, [1929] S.C.R. 630; *David v. Arnott-Smith Timber Co.*, [1952] B.C.J. No. 27, 7 W.W.R. (N.S.) 306 (S.C.).

42 S.Q. 1991, c. 64, Art. 1379 C.C.Q ("C.C.Q.").

43 Article 1432 C.C.Q.

show that the adhering party otherwise knows of these terms.[44] Third, a clause that is illegible or incomprehensible to a reasonable person will be considered null unless the drafting party can show that the clause was adequately explained to the adhering party.[45] Finally, Quebec law states that an abusive clause in a contract of adhesion will be found to be null, or the obligation arising from such a clause will be reduced.[46] An abusive clause is a clause which is excessively or unreasonably detrimental to the adhering party.

Concerns about the enforceability of standard form agreements can largely be addressed by the organization demonstrating that it has made a reasonable effort to bring the terms of the contract to the attention of the adhering party prior to the this party's acceptance of these terms.

Onerous or unusual terms should be brought to the Internet user's attention, such as by highlighting them in separate sections or requiring individual acceptance, *e.g.*, by click-box, in order to demonstrate the Internet user's intention to be bound by those specific terms. To ensure the enforceability of Web policies, it is particularly important that all of the terms are readable before or at the time of acceptance. It is therefore recommended that Web policies and terms not be buried deep in the Web site or cross-referenced to other web pages or documents that the Internet user has not seen before entering the Web site or agreeing to the Web policy and its terms.

In light of the rapidly changing Internet and e-commerce world, and the surrounding legal environment, Web policies may need to be updated and changed on a regular basis. When drafting an agreement that refers to or incorporates the terms of a Web policy that may be unilaterally amended or replaced in the future, one needs to weigh the needs of the party creating the policy against the risks of unenforceability. As an alternative, the related agreement's term may be made shorter such that upon renewal of the agreement, both parties have the opportunity to review and agree to a new policy, for which additional consideration will have been given and received.

---

[44] Article 1435 C.C.Q.

[45] Section 1436 C.C.Q.

[46] Section 1437 C.C.Q.

PART 4

REGULATORY ISSUES

Contracts concluded over the Internet are subject to the same form requirements as contracts concluded in other media. The form requirements of various contracts may be found in a province's sale of goods legislation,[1] its consumer protection legislation,[2] or its unfair business practices legislation.[3]

Web-related activities involving regulated industries, such as financial services, pharmaceuticals, gambling, tobacco and alcohol, may be subject to numerous federal, provincial and territorial laws as well as self-regulatory policies and controls.

---

[1] For Ontario, *Sale of Goods Act*, R.S.O. 1990, c. S.1; for British Columbia, *Sale of Goods Act*, R.S.B.C. 1996, c. 410; for Nova Scotia, *Sale of Goods Act*, R.S.N.S. 1989, c. 408; for Alberta, *Sale of Goods Act*, R.S.A. 2000, c. S-2; for Saskatchewan, *Sale of Goods Act*, R.S.S. 1978, c. S-1; for Manitoba, *Sale of Goods Act*, C.C.S.M. c. S10; for New Brunswick, *Sale of Goods Act*, R.S.N.B., 1973, c. S-1; R.S.N.L. 1990, c. S-6; for Yukon, *Sale of Goods Act*, R.S.Y. 2002, c. 198; for the Northwest Territories & Nunavut, *Sale of Goods Act*, R.S.N.W.T. 1988, c. S-2; for Prince Edward Island, *Sale of Goods Act*, R.S.P.E.I. 1988, c. S-1; for Quebec, arts. 1708 to 1805 of the *Civil Code of Quebec* (collectively "*Sale of Goods Acts*").

[2] Quebec has its own *Consumer Protection Act*, R.S.Q. c. P-40-1 and the sale of goods is also dealt with in arts 1708-1805 of the *Civil Code of Quebec:* See for Ontario, *Consumer Protection Act, 2002*, S.O. 2002, c. 30, Sch. A; for British Columbia, *Consumer Protection Act*, R.S.B.C. 1996, c. 69; for Nova Scotia *Consumer Protection Act*, R.S.N.S. 1989, c. 92; for Alberta, *Fair Trading Act*, R.S.A. 2000, c. F-2; for Saskatchewan, *Consumer Protection Act*, S.S. 1996, c. C-30.1; for Manitoba, *Consumer Protection Act*, C.C.S.M. c. C200; for New Brunswick, *Consumer Product Warranty and Liability Act*, S.N.B. 1978, c. C-18.1; for Newfoundland, *Consumer Protection Act*, R.S.N.L. 1990, c. C-31; for Yukon, *Consumers Protection Act*, R.S.Y. 2002, c. 40; for the Northwest Territories & Nunavut, *Consumer Protection Act*, R.S.N.W.T. 1988, c. C-17; for Prince Edward Island, R.S.P.E.I. 1988, c. C-19 (collectively "consumer protection legislation").

[3] Typical is the Ontario *Sale of Goods Act*, R.S.O. 1990, c. S.1, s. 1 which reads "goods means all chattels personal, other than things in action and money, and includes emblements, industrial growing crops, and things attached to or forming part of the land that are agreed to be severed before sale or under the contract of sale". See also the *Sale of Goods Acts* for British Columbia R.S.B.C. 1996, c. 410, s.1, "goods"; Alberta R.S.A. 2000, c. S-2, s. 1(h), "goods"; Saskatchewan R.S.S. 1978, c. S-1, s. 2(1)(h), "goods"; Manitoba C.C.S.M. c. 510, s.1, "goods"; New Brunswick R.S.N.B. 1973, c. S-1, s. 1(1), "goods"; Nova Scotia R.S.N.S. 1989, c. 408, s. 2(h), "goods"; Newfoundland R.S.N. L. 1990, c. S-6, s. 2(1)(i), "goods"; Yukon R.S.Y. 2002, c. 198, s. 1(1) "goods"; Northwest Territories R.S.N.W.T. 1988, c. S-2, s. 1(1), "goods"; Prince Edward Island R.S.P.E.I. 1988, c. S-1, s. 1(h) "goods".

For example, the *Canadian Code of Advertising Standards*, the Canadian Marketing Association's *Code of Ethics and Standards of Practice* and the Canadian *Code of Practice for Consumer Protection in Electronic Commerce*, establish business practices with respect to e-mail advertising or soliciting.

It is important that an organization structure its Web policies to ensure compliance with the regulatory requirements of its industry.

10

CONSUMER PROTECTION

Web-related activities involving consumers or consumer transactions are subject to consumer protection laws. In particular, the provinces of Alberta, Manitoba, Nova Scotia and Ontario have enacted legislation dealing with requirements for Internet contracts with consumers. Consumer protection legislation in those provinces creates particular obligations that regulate consumer contracts concluded over the Internet. Thus, a supplier concluding an agreement over the Internet must disclose certain information to the consumer, and give the consumer an explicit opportunity to correct any entries into the computer before concluding the contract.[1] After the contract is concluded, the supplier must transmit a copy of the contract to the consumer.[2] The penalty for violating any of these conditions is the voidability of the contract by the consumer within seven days of receiving his or her copy of the contract. If the supplier does not provide the consumer with a copy of the contract, the consumer may void the contract within 30 days of the agreement.[3]

I. ONTARIO

In Ontario, the *Ontario Consumer Protection Act, 2002*[4] (in this section, the "Ontario *CPA*"), which was enacted as Schedule A of Ontario's *Consumer Protection Statute Law Amendment Act,* applies to consumer transactions if either the consumer or the person engaging in the transaction with the consumer (*i.e.*, the supplier or its agent) is located in Ontario when the transaction takes place. "Consumer transactions" mean any act or instance of conducting business or other dealings with a consumer, including a consumer agreement. "Consumer agreement" is defined as an

---

1 Ontario *Consumer Protection Act 2002*, S.O. 2002, c. 30, Sch. A, s. 38; Alberta *Internet Sales Regulation,* Alta. Reg. 81/2001, s. 4; Manitoba *Consumer Protection Act*, C.C. S.M. c. 6200, s. 129; Nova Scotia *Internet Sale Contract Regulations*, N.S. Reg. 91/2002, s. 3.

2 Ontario *Consumer Protection Act,* s. 39; Alberta *Internet Sales Contract Regulation,* Alta. Reg. 81/2001, s. 5; Nova Scotia *Internet Sales Regulation*, N.S. Reg. 91/2002, s. 5.

3 Ontario *Consumer Protection Act,* s. 40; Alberta *Internet Sales Contract Regulation*, Alta. Reg. 81/2001, s. 6; Manitoba *Consumer Protection Act*, s. 130; Nova Scotia *Internet Sales Regulation*, N.S. Reg. 91/2002, s. 6.

4 S.O. 2002, c. 30, Sch. A, s. 38. *Computer Servicenters Inc. v. Beacon Mfg. Co.* 328 F. Supp. 653 (D.S.C. 1970), affd 443 F.2d 906 (4th Cir. S.C. 1971); *Liberty Financial Management Corp. v. Beneficial Data Processing Corp.* 670 S.W. 2d 40 (Mo. Ct. App. 1984).

agreement between a supplier (or its agent) and a consumer by which the supplier agrees to supply goods or services (including any right, entitlement or benefit) for payment. Payment can be consideration of any kind, including an initiation fee. It is likely that licenses of intellectual property to consumers, such as software licenses, will be included within the scope of the Ontario *CPA*.

The Ontario *CPA*, which covers more than just Web agreements, is intended to protect consumers, meaning individuals acting for personal, family or household purposes and not business purposes. The Ontario *CPA* applies to applicable consumer transactions notwithstanding any agreement to contract out of the provisions of the Ontario *CPA*, such as by way of a governing law, exclusion or waiver clause.

The Ontario *CPA* will not apply to certain types of transactions, such as:

- transactions dealing with real property (except time share agreements); and
- transactions which are already regulated under other statutes, such as securities, investments, financial products or services, insurance, public utilities and professional services.

The Ontario *CPA* contains a number of provisions directed specifically to transactions conducted over the Internet. The Ontario *CPA* defines an "Internet agreement" as a consumer agreement formed by text-based Internet communications. It is likely that an agreement formed over a private network or Intranet, would not be considered to constitute an Internet agreement. The Internet agreement provisions are in addition to other requirements in respect of consumer agreements generally, and apply only if the consumer's total payment obligation, excluding the cost of borrowing, exceeds an amount to be prescribed in the regulations.

For those Internet agreements to which the Ontario *CPA* does apply, the Ontario *CPA* requires, among other things, that suppliers, including their agents:

- prior to entering the agreement, disclose certain information (to be set out in the regulations) to consumers, in an accessible, retainable and printable manner;
- immediately prior to entering the agreement, provide consumers with an express opportunity to accept or decline the Internet agreement and to correct errors; and
- subsequent to entering the agreement, provide consumers with a written copy of the Internet agreement within a certain time period (to be set out in the regulations).

The written copy requirement for the Internet agreement will likely be satisfied by using an electronic version as a result of the new e-commerce legislation (such as the Ontario *Electronic Commerce Act, 2000*). That statute states that a legal requirement that a person provide information or a document in writing to another person is satisfied by the provision of the information or document in an electronic form that is:

(1) accessible by the other person so as to be usable for subsequent reference; and
(2) capable of being retained by the other person.

However, the Ontario government may make regulations governing the application of the e-commerce legislation to the Ontario *CPA*.

The Ontario *CPA* enables a consumer to back out of an Internet agreement that she/he has entered, within 30 days, if she/he does not receive a copy of it. As well, the consumer can cancel the contract within seven days after receiving a copy if the supplier did not comply with the disclosure requirement and acceptance procedure.

The Ontario *CPA* also provides for regulations to specify particular terms to be included in Internet agreements and to deem when an Internet agreement shall have been delivered to the consumer. It is important to note that the Ontario *CPA* may apply to all types of consumer transactions, regardless of the medium used. In addition to the express provisions in the Ontario *CPA* dealing with Internet agreements, online consumer transactions might also be subject to other provisions of the Ontario *CPA*, such as, those dealing with:

- future performance agreements, *i.e.*, those consumer agreements in respect of which delivery, performance or payment in full is not made when the parties enter the agreement; and
- remote agreements, *i.e.*, those consumer agreements entered into when the consumer and supplier are not present together.

One potential problem with the Ontario *CPA* is that it is not clear how amendments to Internet agreements will be handled. If an Internet agreement, as is often the case, permits the supplier to unilaterally amend the terms, it is uncertain whether the supplier will have to comply with the disclosure, acceptance and delivery requirements of the Ontario *CPA* each time an amendment is made. In *Kanitz v. Rogers Cable Inc.*,[5] a case decided prior to the enactment of the Ontario *CPA*, the Ontario Superior Court upheld a supplier's agreement that permitted it to unilaterally

5 [2002] O.J. No. 665 (S.C.J.).

amend the contract terms at any time by providing notice via its Web site, or by electronic or postal mail. However, pursuant to the new ss. 7 and 8 of the Ontario *CPA*, one cannot contract out of substantive and procedural rights under the Act and the right to commence a class action under the *Class Proceedings Act, 1992*.[6]

II. QUEBEC

Although Quebec has not passed legislation specifically regulating merchants operating on the Internet, merchants are nonetheless regulated by the provisions of Quebec *Consumer Protection Act*.[7] An example of this issue is that of the "itinerant merchant" provisions. Under this Act, an itinerant merchant is defined as a merchant who, elsewhere than at its address, solicits a particular consumer for the purpose of entering into a contract or enters a contract with a consumer.[8] Under this broad definition, a company that sends e-mail soliciting a particular customer located in Quebec to enter into an agreement via the company's Web site may qualify as an itinerant merchant. Quebec's *Consumer Protection Act*[9] requires itinerant merchants to obtain a licence before soliciting business in Quebec and requires any such itinerant merchants to post security (*i.e.* a bond) in order to request payment of goods prior to their receipt by the consumer.[10] Many existing Web site based businesses either do not know or simply ignore this legal requirement.

III. VOLUNTARY GUIDELINES

The *Principles of Consumer Protection for Electronic Commerce: A Canadian Framework*[11] were developed as a voluntary guideline to be used throughout Canada, applying traditional contract law concepts in the realm of e-commerce. Principle 2 deals with contract formation, stating that vendors should take reasonable steps to ensure that the consumer's agreement to contract is fully informed and intentional. This principle summarises the basic rules of contract formation:

---

6 S.O. 1992, c. 6.

7 R.S.Q. s. P-40.1.

8 *Ibid.*, s. 55.

9 *Ibid.*

10 *Ibid.*, ss. 59, 60. No corresponding obligations to post security seem to exist in the Canadian provinces.

11 Prepared by the Working Group on Electronic Commerce and Consumers (Industry Canada: Ottawa, 1999). See also section 4.5.4 of this letter.

2.1 Vendors should take reasonable steps to ensure that consumers are aware of their rights and obligations under the proposed contract before they agree to the contract or provide payment information.
2.2 Vendors should make clear what constitutes an offer, and what constitutes acceptance of an offer, in the context of electronic sales transactions.

11

LANGUAGES ISSUES

A regulatory issue that is unique to the Province of Quebec is that raised by the application of the *Charter of the French Language*[1] to pre-printed agreements. For example, the *Language Charter* states that contracts containing printed standard clauses, as well as the documents accessory to these contracts, must be drafted in French unless it is the express wish of the parties that they be drafted in another language.[2] In this context, the term "printed" should be understood as including documents available electronically on the Web. Contracts may be bilingual or, in the alternative, be drafted in English only provided that a clause is added to the end of the agreement indicating the wishes of the parties. In such a case, however, a French version of the agreement must be available (*i.e.*, a French version must have been prepared) at the time of entering into the agreement so that a choice of language truly exists for the adhering party. Other language requirements also apply to Web sites as outlined below.

As with all contracts that are generally prepared for use in Canada, consideration should be given to ensuring compliance with the Quebec *Language Charter*.[3] Given the likelihood that a Web site may be accessed by persons in Quebec, Web policies should also contain an English language clause.

Web Site Administration and other corporate policies should state clearly that language issues must be considered whenever drafting contractual terms which may be entered into by residents of the Province of Quebec, or whenever a corporation or entity having an establishment in the Province of Quebec offers information on its products or services through its Web site.

---

1 R.S.Q. c. C-11 ("*Language Charter*").

2 Section 55 of *Language Charter*.

3 *Ibid.*

I. THE REQUIREMENTS OF THE CHARTER OF THE FRENCH LANGUAGE

A. Agreements

If the party who drafted the agreement has an establishment in Quebec, s. 55 of the *Language Charter* will find application. This section states that "[c]ontracts pre-determined by one party, contracts containing printed standard clauses and the related documents must be drawn up in French. They may be drawn up in another language as well at the express wish of the parties."

Online agreements are "pre-determined" agreements containing standard clauses and are therefore subject to this requirement. The Office québécois de la langue française[4] (the "OQLF") has taken the position that, in such a case, an English version of the agreement may be used provided that a French version is available to the customer at the time of entering into the agreement[5] and provided that the English version of the agreement contains a choice of language clause. Such a clause could read as follows:

> The parties hereto have expressly requested that this agreement and all documents related thereto be drafted in English. Les parties aux présentes ont expressément requis que la présente convention et tous les documents y afférents soient rédigés en langue anglaise.

Additional provisions of the *Language Charter* also apply to various other documents such as warranty certificates, for example; however, an examination of these issues is beyond the scope of this book.

Please note also that in the case of agreements with consumers, Quebec's *Consumer Protection Act* provides that, in the case of inconsistencies between the French and English versions, the version most favourable to the consumer will apply.

B. Intranet

Section 4 of the *Language Charter* states that "workers have a right to carry on their activities in French". In addition, s. 41 of the *Language*

---

4 The OQLF is the regulatory body in charge of administering the Charter, while the Commission de la langue française is the administrative body in charge of prosecuting offences under the Charter.

5 Online: <http://www.olf.gouv.qc.ca>.

Charter provides that every employer shall draw up its written communications to its staff in French. Consequently, if the Intranet is used by an employer as a means of communication to its staff, the employer should adopt a policy of making all such communications available in French.

C. Web Sites

Most companies established in the Province of Quebec are aware of the various obligations imposed on them by the *Language Charter* notably in terms of the "francisation" of enterprises in general. However, all companies having an address in the Province of Quebec and advertising products sold in Quebec on their company's Web site should also beware of the provisions of the Charter as they apply to Web sites. This was highlighted by a decision of the Court of Quebec in *Attorney General of Quebec v. Hyperinfo Canada Inc.*[6] According to the court in *Hyperinfo*, such Web sites will have to be in French. A version of the Web site in another language may also exist, but the French version must be given at least equal prominence. This principle applies equally to Web sites directed mostly or entirely at customers outside the Province of Quebec, as long as the products are in fact sold in Quebec (whether these sales are made through the Web site or not).

This decision is based on s. 52 of the *Language Charter* which states that "[c]atalogues, brochures, folders, commercial directories and any similar publications must be drawn up in French". According to regulations enacted pursuant to the *Language Charter*, such documents may also be in two separate versions, one exclusively in French and the other exclusively in another language (not just English), provided that the material presentation of the French version is available under no less favourable conditions of accessibility and quality than the version in the other language.[7]

The OQLF, in its policy relating to Web sites, has taken the position that: (a) s. 52 of the *Language Charter* applies to Web sites, when they are of a commercial character; and (b) s. 52 of the *Language Charter* applies to any enterprise having an address in Quebec. It is this position that was upheld by the court in *Hyperinfo*.

A company operating a Web site in a language other than French may invoke, as possible defences against a complaint of violation of s. 52

---

6 (November 1, 2001), Hull 550-61-000887-014 9 (C.Q.) (unreported).

7 *Regulation Respecting the Language of Commerce and Business*, R.R.Q., c. C-11, r. 9.01, s. 10.

of the *Language Charter*, that: (a) the company does not have an address in Quebec; (b) the Web site does not contain commercial advertising; (c) the products advertised are not sold in Quebec; (d) the Web site is not owned or operated by or on behalf of the company; or (e) the company is covered by one of the exceptions provided in the Charter.

To invoke this last defence, the company will have to prove that it is covered by exceptions set out in the *Language Charter* and which are dictated by the type of business carried by the company, or by its religious, political or cultural nature. The *Language Charter*'s requirements regarding language may not apply to, for example, advertising carried in news media that publish in a language other than French, or to messages of a religious, political, ideological or humanitarian nature if such messages are not expressed for a motive profit.

Please note, however, that the company could not proffer the argument that the users of the Web site implicitly agree to use an English language Web site. The court, in *Hyperinfo*, also held that as s. 52 of the *Language Charter* is a rule of public order (a civil law concept), it cannot be waived contractually.

Please note that the OQLF itself states that it will not usually act of its own initiative, but will often act following receipt of a complaint from a member of the public.

If a company decides to offer a translated version of its Web site in French, it must keep in mind that the French version of the Web site must present ease of access and its importance must be at least equivalent to the English (or other language) version. The forms available on the Web site must also be translated. In addition, the French version of the Web site will need to be upgraded on an on-going basis, to reflect the changes made to the English (or other language) version.

It is unclear whether the use of a link to the French translation from the existing English (or other language) Web site of the company will be sufficient to fulfil the requirement that the French version be as prominent as the English (or other language) version. To our knowledge, the OQLF has not made any public statements on this issue. However, the OQLF has stated (although not consistently) that the *Language Charter* will only be applied to online commercial advertising of products or services that are sold in Quebec. We believe it is therefore possible to infer that the OQLF would accept a link to a translated French version of the site from the general English version of the Web site on the basis that this French version covers all products sold in Quebec. Please note that the link itself must be in French (or be bilingual with French given at least equal prominence). The link to the French version should be clearly visible (and functioning) and the French version must fulfill all other requirements of the *Language Charter*.

The most prudent course of action would be to modify the first page of the Web site to be a simple welcoming page on which the user will chose the language in which it wishes to pursue its exploration of the site. Many Canadian companies have in fact adopted this practice.

Please note that the use of trade-marks may also present a certain challenge to companies using such trade-marks on their Web sites.

The *Language Charter* states that the use of a trade-mark (in any language) on the Web site will be allowed if the trade-mark is a "recognized trade-mark within the meaning of the Trade-Marks Act",[8] providing no French version has been registered (according to the regulations adopted pursuant to the *Language Charter*).[9] If a French version of the mark has been registered, the French version must be used on the French version of the site. It remains unclear whether an unregistered mark which has actually been used by the company in Canada to distinguish its wares or services could arguably be a "recognized trade-mark" under the *Language Charter*.

II. RISKS

When the OQLF takes the position that an enterprise has an address in Quebec and advertises through its Web site products that are made available for sale in Quebec, it may enforce its position on the applicability of the *Language Charter* to the Web site in two ways: (a) through the imposition of requirements related to obtaining a francization certificate (and withholding this mandatory certificate should there be a failure to comply); or (b) through the imposition of fines.

A. The Francization Certificate

Enterprises doing business in Quebec which have more than fifty employees in Quebec have an obligation to obtain a "francization certificate", according to criteria and conditions set out by the OQLF, which may include the obligation to make available a French version of the Web site.

---

8 *Trade-Marks Act*, R.S.C. 1985, c. T-13.

9 Section 13(4) of the *Regulation of the Language of Commerce and Business*, R.R.Q. c. C-11, r. 9.01 (the "Regulation").

B. Fines

In cases where there is an infringement, the OQLF could decide to invoke the penal provisions of the *Language Charter*, and impose fines ranging from $500 to $1,400 for a first offence to $1,000 to $7,000 for subsequent convictions. The OQLF's past practice has been to file a single complaint at a time when it judges a Web site to be in violation of the *Language Charter*.

Should the OQLF take the position that a company has a non-compliant Web site and an address in Quebec, it would, upon receiving a complaint and after conducting an investigation, require this company to make available a French version of the Web site and, should the company refuse to comply, impose fines as outlined above.

C. Public Image

If an organization fails to provide a French version of its Web site, it will also run the risk of having this practice exposed and of, consequently, causing harm to its public image in the Province of Quebec.

12

MARKETING AND ADVERTISING

The fact that the Internet is a global network raises the possibility that an organization's Web site may be accessed by users in different jurisdictions and, consequently, that the marketing and advertising of the organization's products or services on its Web site will be subject to numerous local laws, by-laws, regulations, standards and policies regulating advertising.

For example at the federal level in Canada, the *Competition Act*[1] is the major federal statute with broad application to all forms of advertising, including misleading advertising and deceptive trade practices, in all media. The Act includes a general prohibition against making any false or misleading statement to the public for the purpose of promoting a business interest. The *Competition Act* makes this a criminal offence, if done knowingly (deliberately) or recklessly and, if not done knowingly or recklessly, provides for civil sanctions including cease and desist orders and monetary penalties. In addition to the general prohibition of misleading advertising as a civil matter, the *Competition Act* includes a number of specific civil provisions including:

- a prohibition against making any statement or warranty concerning the performance of a product that is not supported by a proper and adequate test;
- a prohibition against misleading regular price claims;
- a prohibition against misusing testimonials and performance tests; and
- disclosure and other requirements for promotional contests.

The *Consumer Packaging and Labelling Act*[2] and the regulations made thereunder, and the *Food and Drugs Act*[3] and the regulations made thereunder, regulate the advertising of certain kinds of products. There is also specific regulation for products in particular industries. For example, the *Tobacco Act*,[4] regulates the advertising of tobacco. The *Criminal Code*[5] includes anti-lottery and gaming provisions. Other federal laws that

---

1 R.S. 1985, c. C-34 ("*Competition Act*").

2 R.S.C. 1985, c. C-38.

3 R.S.C. 1985, c. F-27.

4 S.C. 1997, c. 13.

5 R.S.C. 1985, c. C-46.

may impact advertising in Canada, include *PIPEDA*, the *Telecommunications Act*[6] and the *Broadcasting Act*.[7]

On the provincial level, consumer protection and business practices statutes of general application within a province may apply. For example, in the Province of Ontario the *Business Practices Act*[8] prohibits a detailed list of unfair practices, including false, misleading or deceptive consumer representations and unconscionable consumer representations. Specialized legislation governs advertising by certain industries. For example: in Ontario, the *Motor Vehicle Dealers Act*[9] includes provisions dealing with false, misleading or deceptive advertising by motor vehicle dealers; and the *Consumer Protection Act* requires specific disclosure when advertising the cost of borrowing. In the Province of Quebec, the *Act Respecting Lotteries, Publicity Contests and Amusement Machines*[10] and the regulations adopted thereunder govern promotional contests. Municipal by-laws may also affect advertising practices, for example by requiring public advertising by auctioneers to disclose the auctioneer's name and business address.

Compliance with privacy laws, as discussed above, should also be considered with respect to the collection, use and disclosure of any personal information.

Some of the industry regulations that may apply in Canada include: the Canadian Association of Broadcasters (CAB) Broadcast Code for Advertising to Children, 1988, the CAB Code of Ethics, 1989,[11] and the Canadian Broadcasting Corporation Advertising Standards, 1993. As well, compliance with various self-regulatory codes including the *Canadian Code of Advertising Standards*,[12] need to be considered.

---

6 S.C. 1993, c. 38.
7 S.C. 1991, c. 11.
8 R.S.O. 1990, c. B. 18.
9 R.S.O. 1990, c. M. 42.
10 R.S.Q. c. L-6.
11 See online: <http://www.cab-acr.ca/english/social/codes/default.shtm>.
12 See online: <http://www.adstandards.com/en>.

13

GAMBLING, LOTTERIES, BETTING AND CONTESTS

Online gambling, lotteries, betting and contests raise different issues than other commercial contracts. The primary regulation of gambling, lotteries and betting is to be found in the *Criminal Code,*[1] while contests, unless they meet a battery of requirements, are considered a form of lottery. Gambling, lotteries, betting and contests are therefore subject to more regulation than other types of e-commerce. Accordingly, in addition to setting out the restrictions of the *Criminal Code*, here we will set out the conditions necessary to comply with provincial legislation for Internet gambling and lotteries, for betting and finally for contests, in order to assist organizations where such activities could be contemplated in adopting a policy setting out the applicable rules. This description of the applicable rules should not be considered comprehensive, and legal counsel should be consulted before undertaking any such activity. In addition, any policy adopted in this respect should also include rules as to when the advice of legal counsel should be sought.

I. INTERNET GAMBLING AND LOTTERIES

The regulation of gambling and lotteries in Canada, is the fruit of a compromise between the provincial and the federal governments. The federal government's power to regulate gambling and lotteries originates in its criminal law power under s. 91(27) of the *Constitution Act, 1867,*[2] and the peace, order and good government residual power in s. 91 of the same Act. While the federal government regulates the moral and criminal aspects of gambling and lotteries, it has explicitly carved out exceptions allowing the provinces to licence certain aspects of legal gambling and participating in lotteries (hereafter "gaming") and run lotteries.

A. Prohibitions

Canada's approach to gaming reflects a division in the popular perception as to the role of gaming in society. Compulsive gaming is an

---

1 R.S.C. 1985, c. C-46.

2 (U.K.), 30 & 31 Vict., c. 3, reprinted in R.S.C. 1985, App. II, No. 5.

important social ill afflicting a small segment of the population, but to many, infrequent gaming may provide a relatively harmless occasional pastime. The Canadian approach to gaming is further complicated by the extent to which the provinces and many charitable institutions rely on various forms of gaming to raise money.

The *Criminal Code* proscribes a variety of related behaviour that can, in the aggregate, be considered either gaming, or necessary for running a gaming establishment. Among these are several that apply only to bricks-and-mortar establishments. We will only consider those provisions that are applicable to gaming over the Internet.

In order to prohibit gaming, many of the actions necessary to run gambling or a lottery are prohibited by the *Criminal Code*. For example, in order to prevent the dissemination of limit information about gambling and lotteries, advertising or publishing in conjunction with gaming is prohibited.[3] Similarly, selling cards or tickets for a game of chance or of admission to a game of chance is illegal.[4] Sending or transferring property in conjunction with a game of chance is also illegal, thereby preventing any legal distribution of prizes.[5] The conduct or managing of a game of chance is proscribed as well.[6]

These provisions effectively criminalise lottery-based games played on the Internet.[7] In addition, the *Criminal Code* also proscribes games such as craps, poker and blackjack, where there is both a skill and a chance component. It is illegal to charge participants for any game of chance or of mixed chance and skill where a participant may win a prize.[8]

Finally, for good measure, the *Criminal Code* prohibits anyone from receiving a lot, card or ticket of the sort used for games of pure chance or of mixed chance or skill.[9]

B. Exceptions

The *Criminal Code* sets out two types of exceptions to the rules above. The first of which is if a licensing system run by the province exists to regulate any game that is not operated on or through a computer, video device or slot machine, or a dice game. This system dispenses

---

3 R.S.C. 1985, c. C-46, s. 206(1)(a).

4 *Ibid.*, s. 206(1)(*b*).

5 *Ibid.*, s. 206(1)(*c*).

6 *Ibid.*, s. 206(1)(*d*).

7 By lottery-based game is a game is where the award of a prize is based solely on chance, independent of any skill of the player.

8 *Ibid.*, s. 206(1)(*f*).

9 *Ibid.*, s. 206(4).

licenses for charitable or religious organizations and for fairs, amusement parks and exhibitions. However, given the constraints on the types of games these organizations may run, Internet gambling and lotteries are strictly excluded.[10]

The second exception grants the government of a province the right to conduct and manage gaming operations in accordance with any law enacted by its legislature. This second grant of power is broader than the first outlined above, since it includes dice games and games operated on or through a computer, video device or slot machine, such as the ubiquitous video lottery terminals (VLTs) and casinos across Canada.[11]

The necessary corollary is that the only Internet gambling and lotteries legal in Canada are those which are conducted and managed by the province. Any business hoping to enter into this sector must therefore ensure that the province is ultimately the entity in control.

II. BETTING

Betting is also proscribed by the *Criminal Code*.[12] The scope of the provisions prohibiting betting is broad, since betting includes the placing of money on any event taking place both inside and outside Canada.

A. Prohibition

According to the *Criminal Code*, keeping money for people engaged in a bet is illegal,[13] as is recording bets or pools[14] and printing any information to be used in conjunction with betting,[15] This prohibition includes importing into Canada material printed elsewhere or material used to promote betting.[16] Engaging in book-making or pool-selling is likewise illegal[17] as is placing bets on behalf of a third party.[18] Another *Criminal Code* provision prohibits sending any information relating to betting through any means of communication.[19] Finally, assisting anyone in

10 *Ibid.*, s. 207(4)(*c*).
11 *Ibid.*, s. 207(4)(*c*).
12 *Ibid.*, s. 201-204.
13 *Ibid.*, s. 202(1)(*c*).
14 *Ibid.*, s. 202(1)(*d*).
15 *Ibid.*, s. 202(1)(*f*).
16 *Ibid.*, s. 202(1)(*g*).
17 *Ibid.*, s. 202(1)(*e*).
18 *Ibid.*, s. 203.
19 *Ibid.*, s. 202(1)(*i*).

anything that is considered an offence under these provisions of the *Criminal Code* is also considered an offence.[20] However, the mere act of placing a bet is not proscribed by the *Criminal Code.*

The *Criminal Code* also sets out several exceptions to the application of the laws proscribing gambling. One of these exceptions provides placing bets through the agency of a pari-mutuel system on running, trotting or pacing horse races is not illegal under ss. 201 through 204 of the *Criminal Code*. This system of betting remains highly regulated by the federal government under the *Pari-mutuel Betting Supervision Regulations.*[21]

B. Pari-mutuel Betting Supervision Regulations

Pari-mutuel betting is a specific type of betting that occurs for horse races, where the money bet on the race is split between the top three winners of a horse race according to their odds of winning. In Canada, pari-mutuel betting is governed by the Regulations that sets up a system of regulation headed by the Executive Director of the Canadian Pari-mutuel Agency (the "Agency"). An organization cannot conduct any pari-mutuel betting without a permit from the Agency. Under the Regulations, the Agency can only grant a permit to an association that owns or leases a racetrack,[22] or to a company that has contracted to operate the pari-mutuel system from such an association.[23] Any organization wishing to deliver pari-mutuel betting through the Internet that does not already own a racetrack would therefore have to obtain the concession of an existing owner.

Anyone able to seek a permit under the Regulations may also conduct pari-mutuel betting on foreign races. However, to do so, the Agency must grant a permit prior to each race that the applicant would like to conduct betting on.[24] For each application, the Agency will not grant a permit unless the applicant provides written evidence of agreement between the applicant and the organization holding the race setting out types of bets offered, methods of calculation used, and the percentage each organization is to keep of the total.[25]

Generally, the various methods of registering a bet in a pari-mutuel system are organized so that the bets are placed from the site of the

---

20 *Ibid.*, s. 202(1)(*j*).
21 SOR/91-365 ("Regulations").
22 *Ibid.*, s. 5(*c*).
23 *Ibid.*, s. 5(*h*).
24 *Ibid.*, s. 94(*a*).
25 *Ibid.*, s. 94(*c*).

racetrack. However, provisions exist for creation of a telephone pari-mutuel system,[26] the Regulations define a telephone as "any telecommunication device that can be used to record and verify a bet made by an account holder".[27] This definition seems sufficiently broad to include the Internet as a means of communication.

The applicant for telephone betting must ask to be assigned an exclusive "home area" over which this organization has the exclusive right to conduct telephone betting.[28] On the other hand, the organization will not be able to grant accounts to residents outside its home area, except for residents of the Yukon and the Northwest Territories, or residents outside Canada.[29] Any set up of a pari-mutuel betting system over the Internet should therefore clearly outline the relevant geographical area.

The Regulations require that the facilities for a telephone betting system must be verified and authorised by the Agency prior to the beginning of operations.[30] Given the lack of control over the location of bettors who set up accounts exclusively over the Internet, the Agency precludes their use. However, the Agency may allow for betting to take place over the Internet for accounts that have been set up over the telephone.

In conclusion, while it is possible to set up a limited Internet betting system for pari-mutuel betting, this industry is heavily regulated by the government, requiring any potential entrepreneurs to partner with an association owning a race track, and putting limits on the use of the Internet to register bets.

C. Enforcement of Contracts

Despite the fact that many types of gambling, lotteries and betting are proscribed by the *Criminal Code*, the enforcement of gaming contracts entered into in a jurisdiction where such behaviour is legal, may be supported by Canadian courts.[31] This is true even of provinces such as Quebec, which have passed laws stating that such contracts, if entered into in the province, are unenforceable.[32] Canadian courts recognise that other

---

26 *Ibid.*, ss. 76-89.

27 *Ibid.*, s. 2 ("telephone").

28 *Ibid.*, s. 76.

29 *Ibid.*, s. 77(2).

30 *Ibid.*, s. 76(2)(*b*).

31 *Boardwalk Regency Corp. v. Maalouf*, [1992] O.J. No. 26, 6 O.R. (3rd) 737 (C.A.); *MGM Grand Hotel Inc. v. Kiani*, [1997] A.J. No. 1084 (Q.B.); *Resorts International Hotel Inc. v. Auerbach*, [1991] A.Q. No. 2228, 89 D.L.R. (4th) 688 (C.A.).

32 *Resorts International Hotel Inc. v. Auerbach*, *ibid*.

jurisdictions may deal with the problems posed by gambling in different ways, and that international comity requires the recognition and enforcement of foreign decisions. Policies dealing with gaming issues should therefore carefully consider jurisdictional issues taking into account both criminal law and consumer protection legislation.

III. CONTESTS

Unlike gambling, lotteries and betting, contests are not specifically prohibited by the *Criminal Code*. However, from a legal perspective, it is very difficult to draw a distinction between a lottery and a contest. In both cases, the participant provides valuable consideration (in Quebec, one would say renders a prestation) and in exchange, receives a chance to win a prize worth more than the initial prestation. The main difference that a contest is generally run either for promotional purposes, or that the contest itself is incidental to the purchase of a different good or service.

Any contest held in Canada must take care not to contravene the provisions in the *Criminal Code* regarding lotteries. Certain aspects relating to the fairness of contests are also regulated by the federal *Competition Act*. However, contests, as part of the property and civil rights of the province also fall within the jurisdiction of the provinces.[33] So far, only the province of Quebec has enacted any additional rules to regulate the filing of registration, advertising of the contest, the language of the contest documents, the posting of certain security and duties owed to the province.

Entities which offer contests on-line should ensure that their policies clearly state that contest rules must be reviewed by legal counsel or another competent person and that all applicable legislative requirements be followed diligently both before and after the contest.

A general outline of the applicable rules is set out below; however, this outline is not intended to be a comprehensive guide to the conduct of contests in Canada and is only intended as a rough guideline in designing a policy related to contests that an organization may wish to make available over the Internet.

---

[33] *Constitution Act, 1867*, (U.K.), 30 & 31 Vict., c. 3, reprinted in R.S.C. 1985, App. II., No. 5, s. 92(13).

A. Federal Legislation

This section sets out federal rules applicable to contests. In accordance with the applicable principles with respect to the constitution separation of provincial and federal powers, these rules apply in conjunction with applicable provincial rules.

1. Criminal Code

Section 206(1) (*a*) to (*d*) of the *Criminal Code* prohibits games of chance. This has been interpreted by the Supreme Court of Canada as meaning that games of "pure" chance are prohibited.[34] Therefore, a game of both skill and chance would not be prohibited by this provision of the *Criminal Code* (hence the use of a skill testing question in most contests).

The skill-testing question must not be too easy, or it will be found not to be a skill-testing question. It must also not be too difficult for the target audience, to ensure that the contest is administered fairly. In short, the question must be such that a member of the target audience of ordinary intelligence and ordinary knowledge can answer without assistance.

Section 206 (1) (*e*) of the *Criminal Code* prohibits schemes in which someone pays money or provides any valuable security and becomes entitled to a larger sum of money *by reason of the fact that other persons have paid money* under the scheme or have given valuable security. This provision prohibits pyramid schemes, but also contests where, for example, contestants pay a certain price to participate and where the prize is based on the participation of others. It is therefore advisable to ensure that the prizes come out of a pre-determined budget (as opposed to basing it upon participation levels).

Finally, s. (1) 206 (*f*) of the *Criminal Code* prohibits the disposal of any "goods, wares or merchandise" by way of any game or chance or game or mixed chance and skill in which contestants pay money or other valuable consideration. If fees are charged to a customer for subscribing to the specific product that is the object of the contest, it would be advisable to include in the rules of the contest a mechanism allowing the public to participate in the contest without subscribing to any service or purchasing any product, to prevent a court from concluding that the contest was organized in contravention to 206 (1) (*f*) of the *Criminal Code*.

---

34 *R. v. Roe*, [1949] S.C.R. 652, 8 C.R. 135.

In summary, a contest organizer must ensure that the contest includes both an appropriate and fairly administered skill-testing question as well as an appropriate no-purchase method of entry. A policy on the development of contests should therefore also clearly set out those requirements.

2. Competition Act

The *Competition Act* provides that certain information must be disclosed to participants in a contest or other promotion. There must be adequate and fair disclosure of: (a) the number and approximate value of the prizes; (b) the area or areas to which they relate (*i.e.*, regional allocation of prizes); and (c) any fact within the knowledge of the contest organizer that materially affects the chances of winning.

The contest organizer must ensure that all relevant details are disclosed in a reasonably conspicuous manner at a time before the potential participant is inconvenienced in some way or committed to the advertiser's products or services or the contest. For example, eligibility criteria should be disclosed in such advertising, so that a customer does not drive to the branch location only to discover that she/he cannot participate.

In other words, relevant basic information must be conveyed before potential participants are committed to the contest or inconvenienced in some way. The actual information disclosed in any advertisement and the extent of the disclosure varies in each case but must take this principle into account.

Another aspect of the "fair disclosure" requirement is that, if prizes are awarded on the basis of location, the advertisement for the contest should not advertise all prizes available throughout the country without stating clearly that the participants only have a chance of winning the prize offered at their own branch location.

The closing date of the contest should also be disclosed, both in terms of meeting the "fairness" requirement and to define the terms of the contest clearly to the public. These requirements should also be spelled out in any policy dealing with the development of contests.

B. Quebec Contest Legislation

The rules applicable to contests in the Province of Quebec are mostly found under the *Act respecting lotteries, publicity contests and amusement machines*[35] and the *Rules respecting publicity contests.*[36]

The *Quebec Lotteries Act* defines a "publicity contest" as:

> a contest, a lottery scheme, a game, a plan or an operation which results in the awarding of a prize, carried on for the object of promoting the commercial interests of the person for whom it is carried on;

The *Quebec Lotteries Act* states that Quebec's Régie des alcools, des courses et des jeux may make rules regarding such contests, which may include imposing registration and filing requirements and the payment of fees, as well as rules regulating the publicity of such contests.

1. Before the Contest

(a) Contest Notice

The first step to take prior to the launching of a contest, if the total value of the prizes offered exceeds $1,000, is to send the "Publicity Contest Notice" (a prescribed form which must be duly completed) with a nominal filing fee to the *Régie des alcools, des courses et des jeux* (the "Régie"), no less than thirty days before the publicity contest is launched.

The contest organizer must also file any relevant information or document that the Régie may require and comply with all the conditions relating to the publicity contest provided for by the *Quebec Lotteries Rules.*

The *Quebec Lotteries Act* also states that the organization for which the contest is held must, where the total value of the prizes offered exceeds $100, pay to the Régie certain duties contemporaneously with the above-mentioned Publicity Contest Notice. The amount of these duties is specified in the legislation and varies according to the geographical distribution of the participants. These duties are not refundable.

(b) Security

The *Quebec Lotteries Act* states that certain categories of persons will have to post security prior to obtaining the authorisation to offer a contest. For example, according to the *Quebec Lotteries Rules*, a person offering, through a contest, to Quebec residents, a prize which exceeds

---

[35] R.S.Q., c. L-6 ("Quebec Lotteries Act").

[36] R.Q., c. L-6, r. 3.1 ("Quebec Lotteries Rules").

$5,000 in value, or various prizes totalling a value of $20,000 or more, will have to provide security.

The security may be furnished either by filing a letter of security in the form prescribed by the Régie, or by depositing the required amount of money with the Régie or in a trust account with a Canadian financial institution. This security will have to be posted for a period during which the winner can claim his prize, plus an additional 30 days.

(c) Contest Rules

Finally, ten days before the contest is publicised, the contest organizer will have to provide to the Régie the advertisements and the rules and regulations applicable to the contest.

2. Rules of a Contest

The following summarizes the *Quebec Lotteries Rules* with respect to its applicability to contests. The rules of a contest must include: (a) the conditions for entering the contest; (b) the places where the public must deposit or send the contest entry form; (c) the deadline for entering the contest; (d) a description of the method of awarding the prizes; (e) the number and a detailed description of the prizes offered and the value of each prize; (f) the place, date and precise time the prize-winner will be named; (g) the media used to inform the winners of the prizes won; (h) the date, place and deadline for claiming prizes or, where applicable, whether the prize will be delivered to the winner; (i) information that the winner will be selected by a jury, where applicable; (j) the disclaimer that as a minimum the following persons will be excluded in all cases: the person for whom the publicity contest is carried on, his employees, representatives and agents, the members of the jury and the persons with whom they reside; (k) a prescribed text for disputes relating to the contest; and (l) the nature of the skill-testing requirement that a winner has to satisfy in order to claim his prize.

The *Quebec Lotteries Rules* (s. 5 (10)) also require that the following text be inserted in the rules of a contest:

> Any litigation respecting the conduct or organization of a publicity contest may be submitted to the Régie des alcools, des courses et des jeux for a ruling. Any litigation respecting the awarding of a prize may be submitted to the Régie only for the purpose of helping the parties reach a settlement.

3. The Advertising of the Contest

The *Quebec Lotteries Rules* with respect to contest advertising are as follows: (a) the advertising shall not state or imply that any person has won a given prize; (b) the advertising shall not state or imply that any person may enter a contest for the purposes of receiving a prize or being able to win a prize, when in fact all participants receive a prize; (c) the advertising shall state the number of and describe the prizes offered in the contest and their respective value, and shall mention, where applicable, that only one prize is offered or shall specify the smallest and the largest value of the prizes; (d) the advertising shall set out how and where the public may obtain the text of the contest rules; and (d) where participation in a publicity contest requires the purchase of a good or service, the advertising shall set out the nature of the skill-testing requirement that a winner must satisfy in order to claim his prize.

4. After the Contest

The contest organizer will have thirty days after the prize winners are named to inform them of the procedure to follow in order to claim their prizes.

Within 60 days following the date on which the prize winners are named, the contest organizer will have to file a report with the Régie, containing certain information prescribed by the legislation.

The contest organizer must retain all documents, participation forms and other vouchers for the contests for a period of 120 days following the winner selection date.

5. Restrictions on Eligibility

Employees, agents and representatives of the contest organizer cannot participate in the contest.

Finally, in order to avoid potential disputes, the sentence "Judges decisions are final" should be included in the contest rules.

6. Additional Issues

Please note that as previously discussed, both Federal and provincial privacy legislation in Quebec prohibit the collection, use and disclosure of an individual's personal information without the consent of the person concerned, which consent must be obtained for specific purposes. If the contest organizer wishes to use the names of the winners of the contest for the purposes of publicity, for example, it must obtain their consent to do so. This request for consent should also be included in the rules of the contest. Issues relating to the collection, use and disclosure of personal information are further discussed elsewhere in this book.[37]

Please note also that, under Quebec's *Charter of the French Language*,[38] a French version of the contest rules must be made available to participants in Quebec. When made available online, a link should be included from the English version of the contest rules to the French version, to ensure that this French version is made available at the time of entering into the contest.

---

[37] See Part 1 (Chapter 1, Section II), Part 2 (Chapter 4, Section XI) and Part 3 (Chapter 8).

[38] R.S.Q., c. C-11.

INDEX

M

P

R

S

T

W